CHASED BY THE DRAGON
CAUGHT BY THE LAMB

If only the solution to the drug problem was as simple as 'just say "no"'. In this book you will read of Brian's account of his drift into drugs and the catastrophic impact they caused to every part of his life. He spiralled down and hit the bottom. But God was waiting for him there.

This is a well-written, true-life, story that leads you down through drug-dependent despair and raises you up to the hope of a Christ-filled life and a better future. It didn't happen overnight. It didn't happen alone. This book should encourage Christians to walk with people like Brian, to see them continue their lives, prison and drug free.

Peter Walker, Executive Director, Prison Fellowship England and Wales

CHASED BY THE DRAGON CAUGHT BY THE LAMB

The Incredible True Story of a Drug Addict Reborn

BRIAN MORRIS
WITH MARTIN SAUNDERS

Authentic
LIFESTYLE

Copyright © 2003 Brian Morris and Martin Saunders

First published 2003 by Authentic Lifestyle

09 08 07 06 05 04 03   7 6 5 4 3 2 1
Authentic Lifestyle is an imprint of Authentic Media,
9 Holdom Avenue, Bletchley, Milton Keynes, Bucks,
MK1 1QR, UK
and PO Box 1047, Waynesboro GA 30830-2047

British Library Cataloguing in Publication Data
A catalogue record for this book is available from the British
Library

1-86024-435-1

Cover design by David Lund
Print Management by Adare Carwin
Printed and Bound in Denmark by Nørhaven Paperback

ACKNOWLEDGEMENTS

I would like to thank Pauline Lewis for her patience
with me and expert advice and help on this book;
David Waite for his encouragement and input in the
tidying up process.

Thanks also to the Revd W. Kerry Jenkins
for inspiration,
Calvary Full Gospel Church Clydach
for prayers and support,
and my brothers and sisters for their
forgiveness and love.

This book is dedicated to Erika and Sonny Ray.

ONE

12.00 p.m., room 610

It was midday. The sun was streaming through the thin blinds of our Swansea hotel room, ushering in a cold December afternoon, but I was not interested in getting out of bed. I was going through 'cold turkey' because my supply of heroin had run out, and I didn't know where to buy more. I was drifting in and out of a restless sleep. I'd begun to suffer hot and cold sweats two days before, and now my whole body was aching. I had chronic diarrhoea and was struggling to keep down anything I ate or drank for more than a few minutes. When I did manage to string together a few moments of sleep, I was cursed with horrible nightmares. Room 610 of the Forte Crest Hotel had become my own private torture chamber.

It had been three days since I had smoked the last of my heroin. I scratched my bald head and looked over at the snoring figure of my companion Ahmed, curled up under the blankets in the other bed. Would this be the day we would finally get out of this hell? Would today be the day we would sell the drugs and travel back home to Holland?

Suddenly the door burst open, and my heart nearly stopped in shock. Before we could move, a voice shouted to tell us not to. I looked up, and found myself staring down the barrel of a loaded weapon. This was a raid.

Several guns were pointing at both of us. I froze – stunned and devastated – yet somehow I was able to think clearly.

'*I'll get ten years for this*,' was my first consideration.

I knew I had better not give them any lip, or they would use it against me in court, and that would mean more time. Then I took a deep breath, and something even more shattering dawned on me. The faces of my infant son and his mother flashed across my brain. Any chance of a relationship with them had just been destroyed as that door had swung open.

Knowing that any reaction, outburst or struggle could be written down and used as evidence against me, a compulsion to stay calm took over. I realised that my freedom was evaporating fast, if it hadn't gone already. I remembered the time I had been caught with a very small amount of hashish twenty years earlier, and how the police had twisted the evidence then because I had said things I shouldn't have. So now I was determined to be in control of myself. I would not allow the situation to overwhelm me, though I knew the game was up. I was trying desperately to work out how I could cut my inevitable sentence by being as co-operative as possible. I knew this was the end of my drug dealing and I was terrified; shuddering; in a state of total despair.

Ahmed

Ahmed's parents came as Turkish immigrants to Holland when he was only four, so he spoke Turkish and Dutch. He was 22, about five-foot-four inches tall with short dark brown hair, yet despite his size he was a confident young man. He had been dealing in drugs since his early teens, but this had been his first visit to the UK. It had been his persistence and his money that had enabled us to work out our plan, but it had been my long involvement in drug-dealing that had given us the necessary contacts to set it all into operation.

The Turkish dealers in The Hague allowed me to have drugs on credit, until I had built up a debt of 4,000 guilders, about £1,500 at the time. They were beginning to put pressure on me to pay up. Then, unexpectedly, I got a visit from Ahmed. He had been the one who had originally supplied me with heroin for my habit, but he had risen up the ladder since then and had given the business to his younger mates, and it was on them that I now depended for a fix.

He turned up at my flat with a proposition. He asked me if I would go to Morocco to bring hashish back to Holland – with the promise, 'all your debts will be sorted.' I wasn't keen though – I had a young family to think about now, and didn't want to dig myself any deeper into the hole that drugs had put me in. After trying a few times to persuade me with this plan, and getting nowhere, he came back with another one. This time he asked me, 'Brian, will you take some cocaine to your country?' But again I refused.

A few days later, his mates called in and leaned on me a little. They told me that there could be a problem if I didn't pay them soon. The pressure was mounting. I knew that these men could be very dangerous, so I changed my mind and agreed to do it before they decided to lean on me a little too hard.

I was desperate to end the misery that my debt and addiction had caused. It had all seemed so easy at the time. If all had gone according to plan, we would have been back in Holland within forty-eight hours, and I certainly wouldn't have been left aching and shivering in a damp hotel bed.

One big factor made the decision easier: I knew I had an outlet when I got across the Channel. Joe Roberts, an old school acquaintance from Wales, had been phoning me in recent months, asking me to bring drugs over to Britain. He was just over a year older than I was, of medium build, a little under six feet tall with fair, thinning hair. He was not married – maybe divorced, I'm not sure – I hadn't really known him well since our teens. Joe dressed in a casual style: not scruffy, but not smart either.

We'd seen each other a few months before when I was on another dealing trip. We had been two old faces happy to see each other after so long, even though we had never been close mates in the past. I couldn't remember much about him, aside from watermarked memories of us as boys, but I certainly hadn't any reason to mistrust him. He had assured and encouraged me on the telephone that he could shift all the drugs I could bring. I told him I had finished with all that because of my situation with my partner and new baby. He had let it go for a few weeks before he telephoned again, and this time, I was facing a crisis. I couldn't see a way out of my situation. Again, Joe persuaded and encouraged me. 'I can get rid of anything you bring,' he assured. He sounded so convincing that I decided to give it one last shot. After all, how on earth would I find the money to pay off the dealers otherwise?

Joe had approached me in a local pub when I was on my earlier visit. He had known that I was doing business with Ricky, another old 'friend'. Ricky was a short, well-rounded, stocky character who smoked menthol cigarettes non-stop. Over the years, this had caused him to wheeze heavily. He often had to use an inhaler to catch his breath. Sharp and streetwise, he was always on the lookout for a quick buck. However, I wasn't intending to do business with Ricky again, after he'd stitched me up last time. Instead of sending me my proper share of the money, he had been greedy and hadn't paid me in full, so I didn't want him in on this deal.

After hearing from Ricky that I was in the drugs business, Joe had kept asking me to deal directly with him. I never expected to do any more high-risk dealing again, and so at first his pleas fell on deaf ears. But on the other hand, I never expected to be in so much debt. So then his proposal – given weight by the pressure applied by Ahmed's mates – increasingly seemed the only option I had left to get out of the terrible mess I was in.

Coming over

'OK Ahmed,' I conceded, on Ahmed's sixth or seventh visit to my flat, 'I'll do it.'

That evening, early in the December of 1995, I phoned Joe and told him a deal was on. Ahmed arranged at first to bring half a kilo of cocaine, but by the day before we left, he had managed to double it. I phoned Joe again to clear it with him. He sounded really happy with the prospect of more profit. He assured me that he and Jeremy (his contact) had got his end sorted and could sell it all in a day, or maybe two at the most. It was all arranged; all we had to do was arrive undetected.

Intentionally, I gave Joe some false information on the phone. I had implied that we would be coming from Hook van Holland to Harwich. In fact, my plan was to come from Ostend in Belgium to Ramsgate in Kent. I figured that anyone listening to our conversation would be put off our trail – allowing us to arrive safely. (The last thing a sensible dealer would do is speak of his plans on the phone.) All the arrangements had been discussed in terms of 'tapes' for sale, and we took care never to openly mention drugs. The police know all the tricks, and tap in to listen to many unsuspecting people. If they were on to us, I must have come across as very stupid laying out my route on the phone. But this was all part of the plan, and we arrived safely.

We travelled from Ramsgate on the 3 a.m. train to London's Victoria Station, then took the tube to Paddington for the Swansea train. When we finally arrived there, we got a cab to Clydach – six miles away. We pulled up at Joe's house around half past ten in the morning. I knocked on his door while the driver was opening the boot to get out our luggage. Joe opened the door but seemed very surprised to see us. I could see that he was stuck for words when he saw Ahmed getting out of the taxi. It was as if he wasn't expecting us, which I immediately thought was strange. He looked really spooked.

'You can't stay here, the place is being watched by cops,' whispered Joe, obviously nervous. 'You'll have to take the stuff somewhere else until I get things sorted. It's too risky for you to be here.'

Why should it be suddenly risky? It seemed dead around this house. I didn't notice anything suspicious. Only the day before, Joe had told me on the phone that there would be no problem. The 'tapes' that we would be bringing would be moved on in a day and there was plenty of room for us to stay. Now we get here to find a completely different story. After a long and nerve-wracking – although ultimately successful – trip through customs, I couldn't believe this.

I put my foot down: 'We're not going anywhere until we get some food, a shower and some rest.'

Problems

There was no way I was just going to leave Joe's place yet. We had only just got there! Bringing a kilo of cocaine from Holland into Wales had been a massive undertaking. All the arrangements had been made and then, when we'd finally arrived at our destination, we found that they'd been changed at the last moment. It was not something that could be rearranged at a moment's notice. Something was wrong but I was too tired to be suspicious.

Joe's flatmate, an alcoholic named David, stashed the drugs for us. That bought us some time. David had been a neighbour of our family and was my brother Raymond's best friend for years when they were kids. I trusted him completely. I sent my small supply of heroin with the coke to stash, just in case it was true that there were police hiding somewhere nearby.

But I was an addict. A few hours later I needed some heroin badly because I was becoming sick without it. I asked David to get it for me on the grounds that I needed to stay focussed. There was no room for getting sick. After he came back I rushed into the bathroom. I could feel myself getting more sick, and fumbled with the packet in a rush to open it, spilling some of the precious brown powder on the floor. I 'cleaned' it up with the palm of my hand and licked it eagerly. But there was no instant high to be had from that, so I smoked some on silver foil as well. I felt the numbing effect begin to take control. The relief was incredible – the sickness disappeared straight away as my body perversely restored itself through this desperately unhealthy substance. I wrapped up the rest in cling film and stored it inside me just in case the police turned up unexpectedly. Now perhaps I could relax for a while.

I returned from the bathroom, feeling better through the combination of a freshening wash and a good helping of heroin, but was knocked off balance when I reached the living room. Sitting there, whispering with Joe, was none other than Ricky, the dealer who short-changed me last time I was over here. Why was he here, I wondered? Even if he was an old mate, I certainly didn't trust him after the way he had let me down last time.

I looked across at Joe.

'What's he doing here?' I asked.

Ricky butted in, 'You can't keep nothing from me Brian. Me and Joe always work together.'

Nevertheless, Joe had assured me he would not be involved; that he wouldn't even know we were coming. So how was it that he was there? I was getting an uncomfortable feeling. Something was going on – but what were they up to? I walked out of the room feeling a little guilty that I had tried to cut Ricky out of the deal.

'Change money Brian, England money need,' Ahmed explained in his broken English as he passed me on the stairs.

'I'll go and change money for you,' offered Joe enthusiastically.

Ahmed looked a little concerned so I reassured him that it was OK, then watched as he gave Joe a 1,000 guilder note to change at the local bank.

'I'll be back in about half an hour,' Joe shouted up the stairs to me. 'Then I'll make a few phone calls and sort something out.' Joe and Ricky left together and Ahmed and I waited in the house. Joe came back alone with the changed money and revealed that someone was coming later to see the cocaine.

Later that afternoon, two heavy-looking skinheads, both around 30 years old, came to test a sample. These weren't the contacts Joe talked about on the phone, I thought.

'We haven't got long, show us the gear,' grunted the stockier of the two, who had a heavily-tattooed neck.

David, Joe's flatmate, had collected some of the cocaine from the hiding place. I asked Ahmed to bring two grams for them to test. They used their own scales to check the weight. Then they went through the purification process, which involves burning off any impurities, to test the quality of the product.

'It's good stuff!' they granted, finding it to be 80 per cent pure. 'We'll be in touch very soon.'

But as I said, these were not the guys Joe had told me about on the phone before Ahmed and I had left Holland. It seemed like they were a last-minute replacement – perhaps no more than a diversion organised to keep us sweet. We waited and waited until evening but they didn't come back. Joe told us that we would be given a lift into Swansea to find a place to stay. But my mind was going into overdrive wondering what all this garbage was about. Why wasn't it sorted like he told me it would be? Nobody was saying that it was bad gear, so if that wasn't the problem, then what was?

Getting desperate

Joe had organised a lift for us to find a room in Swansea – we took the cocaine with us of course. Because I was irritated by the complications we'd encountered, I decided to be a bit cheeky as we passed the four-star Forte Crest Hotel.

'Let's stay here man,' I said. There was a 'special offer' banner on display that said the price for a twin bedroom was £75 a night instead of the normal £100. Ahmed had brought a few thousand guilders with him and I took advantage of the fact. So, that's where we checked in.

After settling into room 610, I wandered up the stairs to nose around for somewhere to hide the coke. I found a narrow door with a warning sign on it. Checking to see if the coast was clear, I tried the door. It was open! Fumbling in the dark, I found a light switch. A very dim light came on, and I could see a steel staircase about six feet high. I climbed the dusty stairs and put the cocaine behind a large boiler which I found at the top. I was very careful to check that no one was about before I left the boiler room. I hurried back downstairs and was soon back in my room without being seen.

My supply of heroin would last for another twenty-four hours. After that, I knew 'cold turkey' would set in. Where in Swansea could I buy some more? After a shower, I took a walk around some Swansea pubs and bars, but I didn't have the nerve to go in to any of them and start asking questions. I was in a terrible state. It would not be wise to talk about that sort of thing with strangers, as I would almost certainly have brought unwanted attention to who I was and what I was up to. With each passing hour I was getting more desperate, knowing that I would soon start to deteriorate. All I could think of was getting more heroin, because I couldn't function properly without it.

On the morning of the second day Ahmed and I travelled by taxi back to Joe's to see what was happening. We were hoping to clinch the deal, but nothing had developed at all. I asked Joe to get me some heroin to relieve my rapidly deteriorating condition, but he told me that he had tried a few contacts for me and they didn't have any. After a long wait at his house, by which time I was becoming delirious and drifting in and out of sleep, I did manage to get 50 ml of methadone from an addict who had called in to see Joe. It was enough to bring me some much needed relief for about ten hours.

We returned to the hotel, and the following day I persuaded Ahmed to go to Joe's again by taxi to check out the score, as we were both anxious for results. I was too sick to go myself. Of course, it was my job to put the deals into operation not his, and understandably he was angry. He didn't take drugs himself, only sold them – a very smart dealer indeed. He had every right to be livid at me, but we couldn't just wait and hope. He came back from Joe's in the evening, saying he had a chance to sell some and asking me to retrieve the cocaine from the hiding place so he could weigh out a couple of ounces. I staggered up the stairs to the boiler room, checking that no one saw me on the way. It was very hot in the little room and I was worried that the heat might have damaged the cocaine. Checking again that no one was about, I brought the drugs down to our room. I opened the wrapping carefully. I was shaking through a combination of drug deprivation and fear. I was terrified that the package would be damp and messed up, and so I was mightily relieved to find that it was still in perfect condition.

The two guys that brought Ahmed back from Joe's place were Ricky's son Ryan and a guy called Skewen John. It was all getting out of hand with too many strangers involved. By this time though, there was nothing else we could do, so we just hoped and trusted that there would be no problems.

Then another guy turned up – the fellow who was supposed to shift the whole kilo in the first place. This was Jeremy, the contact that Joe had told me about a number of times on the phone, and the reason we'd come over here with the drugs. He arrived while Ahmed was getting the ounce ready for the men waiting in the car. He was a wiry figure, about six feet tall, with long black hair. A shifty, creepy-looking character, his eyes were too close together for my liking. He bought four grams for a sample and promised that he would be back soon.

He didn't come back again.

Ahmed went with Ryan and the fellow named 'Skewen John' to sell the ounce. Meanwhile I was shivering and feeling progressively weaker. I called room service for some beers on Ahmed's tab. Then I 'cooked' up some crack cocaine by heating it like the two skinheads had done. I sucked eagerly at the smoke, desperately hoping to feel relief but only ending up feeling sicker than before. I was a heroin addict and, ultimately, I needed heroin to make me feel better, not a substitute. Nothing would help except heroin, and I badly needed some now.

So now it was the fourth day, and we were still sitting on the rest of the drugs. Ahmed had become increasingly angry as the time passed, telling me that I was a 'useless stupid junkie'. He was right of course, but then how could I have known that Joe would not do what he had told me he would?

Of course, we should have changed hotels each day, and I'm sure I would have smelled a rat if I had not been in such a mess. No junkie is in full control. All I could think about was smoking some heroin on some silver foil, which is known as 'chasing the dragon'. The heated fumes are 'chased' by sucking the anaesthetising smoke through a tube. Not as potent as injecting of course, but once heroin has you in its vice-like grip, you become its slave and will take it any way you can. But with no heroin available to me, and my drug-dealing escapade going seriously off course, something suddenly became very clear to me.

I wasn't chasing the dragon any more. Now the dragon was chasing me . . . and it wanted my life.

12.01 p.m., room 610

Suddenly the door burst open, and my heart nearly stopped in shock. Before we could move, a voice shouted to tell us not to. I looked up, and found myself staring down the barrel of a loaded weapon. This was a raid.

It seemed like the end of the world. I looked over at Ahmed in his bed. He was looking as shocked and dumfounded as me.

'You idiot Brian,' he grumbled loudly in Dutch. 'Crazy Wales people don't know how to do business.'

'Shut it!' growled one of the cops. 'Get out of your beds.'

You don't argue when there are guns pointed at you. Almost a kilo of cocaine was in the case next to my bed where Ahmed had left it the night before, after he had weighed up the ounce. For three nights, it had been stashed in the boiler room on the floor above, but I had not put it back in the hiding place, as I should have. When Ahmed had come back at around 1 a.m., a cocktail of cold turkey and laziness stopped me from getting up to re-stash it.

Numb from shock, I pulled back the blankets.

'Slowly does it boys, so where're the drugs then?' one of the police asked, calmly.

'There, in that case.' I pointed to it on the floor next to my bed.

'Whose case is it?'

'Mine.' I admitted.

One of them picked up the plastic bag in the case and asked. 'What's in this bag then?'

'A kilo of cocaine,' I answered straight out.

He grinned and chuckled triumphantly at the others. 'Had trouble getting rid of it, did you boys?'

I kept my mouth shut. I felt an urge to snatch the bag and fling it out of the window, but there were too many of them. It would not have been a good idea. They would have grabbed me as soon as I made a move; might even have shot me. No, I decided I would rather live. One of them cautioned us and then on went the inevitable handcuffs. The cold steel pressed painfully against the bones in my wrists.

'Ik geef je 60,000 gulden als jij tegen de politie zegt dat ik niets met die zaak te maken heb en dat ik alleen ben gekomen om boodschappen voor de Kerst te doen, ja Brian?'

'Shut up!' said one of the cops as they fastened our wrists tightly with the handcuffs.

Ahmed had pleaded in Dutch for me to cover for him and say that he had nothing to do with the drugs; to say that he was only on a Christmas shopping holiday with me. He offered me £25,000 pounds to say this – a very tempting offer indeed.

But not knowing what to do and thinking that only the truth could help me now, I could only answer, 'I don't know.' Making up a story on the spot means you'll need a very good memory in court. They had found us together in the room with the drugs, and would convict the both of us whatever our stories. That was my reasoning, anyway. Again, as we conversed desperately in Dutch we were told to shut up. It must have irritated them that they couldn't understand what we were talking about. There were about ten cops, some kitted out in black SWAT-style gear. It all seemed like a bad dream because of the withdrawal symptoms I was going through, but this was not a dream, it was solid, down-to-earth reality. It was the most painfully sobering experience I'd had in years.

My mind drifted, but I wasn't so far gone that I couldn't realise what a fool I had been. Joe had been so convincing on the phone. But why had I trusted him? And then, why hadn't I taken the coke back up to the boiler room? This is the end of the line Brian boy, I told myself. You took it too far and now you must pay the price for the life you chose.

I felt drained and humiliated as we were led past the police to the lift. It was even worse as we passed through reception. We were exposed – laid bare – and I felt ashamed, not knowing where to look as the cold, intense gazes of many guests and staff pierced right through us. We were led to a car and taken to the police station just around the corner. Inside five minutes, we had been locked up in the dark, cold, filthy station cells.

Marie Claire

The next three days were the most sobering days of my life. In between questioning, I managed to see a doctor, but he wouldn't give me anything stronger than paracetamol to ease my pain. I curled up under a smelly, coarse blanket, shivering one moment and sweating the next, retching constantly. Later, another doctor was a little more sympathetic. He gave me 15 ml of methadone, but it only slightly eased my condition.

Alone in that cold little cell I had something else to worry about, or rather, someone. When the police raid first took place, he was one of the first things to come into my mind. Now I couldn't stop thinking about him: my two-month old son, Sonny Ray.

I had met his mother, Marie Claire, at a flat above a drug spot where I occasionally bought heroin. She had been lodging there with an English coke dealer and his

wife. Needing money, Marie Claire had asked me if she
could come and clean my house for 25 guilders a time.
She was a very good-looking girl, and at 25 guilders it
was a bargain, so I barely hesitated before agreeing. On
her second cleaning visit, she didn't want to leave. I was
really hoping she would stay but I was fourteen years
older than her and thought better of pushing things in
case I got the brush-off. Finally I became tired and didn't
know what to say. So I just took a hope-fuelled shot in the
dark:

'I'm going to bed, just make yourself at home.'

I got into bed and there was a silence for about five
minutes before I heard her shouting from the living room.

'Can I sleep with you tonight Brian?' she called.

I could not believe my ears. I had not had a girlfriend
for about five years!

I pictured her in my mind now, with her beautiful
wavy hair and melting brown eyes. Five-foot-eight inches tall with an amazingly slender waist, her high cheek-
bones and thick dark eyebrows – from a mix of Moroccan
and Dutch ancestry – enhanced her beauty. She spoke
Dutch, English, Arabic, French and German – so she was
beautiful and smart! What I would have given to be back
in Holland with her.

What would become of her now, I wondered, with our
child to care for? What a fool I had been to leave them
alone with all those hustlers about. How would she cope?
She had psychiatric problems, needing the strong antide-
pressant drug 'Haldol' to control her moods. I'm sure she
had once suffered a nervous breakdown. Now she was
very vulnerable and in danger, and here was I in the cell
of a British police station, staring down a long stretch. I'd
had dreams of us travelling together, especially since with
her around, we'd never have a problem with languages. I

had longed to help her to get off all drugs. I'd longed to get myself clean too. She had pleaded with me not to go on this trip, but I told her that this was a chance to clear my debt, even though I had vowed to stop using and selling drugs. If I could pull off this job, I said, we could start to think about the future. I wanted to look after them, after all, and with the debts clear, I'd really be able to. In reality of course, I couldn't even look after myself.

Just two months earlier, Sonny Ray had been born six weeks premature and had been put on a drip for a week. At the time that she became pregnant, Marie Claire was addicted to smoking crack cocaine and I to smoking heroin and crack, and to snorting coke. When we found out about the pregnancy, I started to undergo a detox programme with methadone, a heroin substitute. We both did our best to stay off drugs for a while. I had been addicted to heroin for about two years, but not heavily. I didn't inject it; I smoked it on silver foil. Cocaine had been my friend for much longer – for fourteen years in fact. While Marie Claire was pregnant we made a decent fist of bringing down our drug intake.

Despite our addictions, we had managed to get everything ready for Sonny Ray's birth. We had a cot, clothes, pram, bath and more. His bedroom was lovely. We had bought the most expensive wallpaper and curtains, and for a while it felt like a fresh start. But soon after he was born, it all went out of control again. Our intake of drugs had increased while Sonny Ray was in hospital. Marie Claire would tell me that she was going to visit her grandmother, but instead she would go to a crack cocaine house where she would hang around for days at a time. At other times she would bring some crack cocaine home and I couldn't resist it. I would join in. Then we would take it in turns to go and purchase some little white 'rocks' of crack

a few street
all, like
We tr

alth deterio-
soon we
don't

TWO

Early days, [illegible] times

I was born on the shortest day of the year, 21st December in 1953. Most people can't remember much about the first couple of years of their lives, but I'm an exception, and it's hardly surprising. My earliest memory, and one that will never leave me, is of a month before my first birthday. I had managed to climb out of my high chair and crawl up to the gas stove, where the family dinner was cooking. I reached up to the chip-pan handle, and pulled the boiling hot chips down over me. My mother had only left me for a moment to hang some clothes on the line: she heard my blood-curdling screams and rushed inside. The sizzling fat had spilled all over my shoulder and my face – it was still cooking on my skin through the clothes. Thinking quickly, despite her horror, she grabbed a cloth and wiped the boiling fat from my face – and I'm sure that's why I'm not facially scarred today. The hot fat on my clothes was a different matter though. It left my shoulder and upper arm scarred for life.

The next six weeks were spent in Chepstow Burns Hospital. I had many hideous nightmares in those first few years – all of which involved burning in fire – and I often woke up screaming. It made me a nervous and troubled child. I still remember my first day at school: I would not let go of my mother's skirt and screamed for her not to leave me there. I was absolutely terrified.

I grew up in a big family, and that's no understatement. It seemed like there were hundreds of us. I had three brothers when I was born: John was the eldest, then Raymond and David. Susan, Wendy and Christopher came after. Seven kids then, and our mam and grandad, in our red-bricked end-of-terrace house in South Wales. But there were more. Our Uncle Dennis and Auntie Valerie lived with us too, and, when he was on leave from the Army, we also had our Uncle Peter there. So in terms of spaciousness, it was hardly the Ritz.

Uncle Ken and Auntie Doreen and six cousins lived on the same terrace only a few doors away – so we saw plenty of them. Auntie Margie and Uncle Pat who also lived nearby often came with our cousins too. Uncle Les and Auntie Iris used to come on visits from Hereford and I would run into Les's arms every time he did, hoping to get sweets.

Dear Grandad, always helped our family in every way he could, despite his own problems. A retired crane driver (he had worked at the famous Mond Nickel Refinery Company in Clydach), he was loved and respected by the local people, and especially by our family – so much so that we all used to call him 'Dad'. He had a heavy snuff addiction and over the years, his nostrils had merged into one hole. The tip hung hook-like over the hole, so that when he blew his nose the hook wiggled back and forth! He had been a proud man, and despite our poverty he always held his head high. Even in the difficult times, he had always been immaculately turned out in his grey pinstripe suits, long brown overcoat, walking stick and elegant Bailey hat. Every child in the area thought that the statue of the German chemical genius,

Ludwig Mond, which stood outside the Nickel Company, was my grandfather Hector Morris. (The long overcoat, walking stick and the Bailey hat did the trick – Mond's statue wore pretty much the same clothes. Moreover, they shared that large hook-like nose!) I used to tell everyone that the statue was of my grandad.

My brothers and I used to play marbles and many other games. My older brothers often made 'bogies' from old pram wheels and planks of wood that we rode recklessly down steep hills. Two large wheels were used at the back and two smaller ones on the front with a piece of wood for the feet and some rope for steering.

But we spent most of our time playing around the nearby railway line. We chased the slow steam trains that chugged past nearby, or we used old cardboard boxes to slide down the slippery grass of the long sloping embankment. Clydach fairground was right next to the line and we were always excited when, twice a year, the fair arrived. It was only a hundred yards from our house!

Often we made bows and arrows from the straight branches of willow trees and played among the cliffs shooting at each other from each side of the line. My brother Raymond made throwing arrows and could throw them up to a hundred yards.

Auntie Valerie used to take us up Glais Mountain to pick wind-berries that Mam would make delicious tarts with. There was a huge rock on the top, which we would sit on to look down on the village and the whole valley – up to the Brecon Beacons and down to the shining sea of Swansea Bay. Other times we all went paddling in the river – catching catfish or 'tickling' trout.

Occasionally, Mam took us to Swansea Bay and we would ride on the Mumbles trams – the first passenger railway in the world.

What I'm trying to say through all these recollections is this: we may have been poor but we had happy times. We didn't have much and often ate dripping sandwiches and porridge oats. There were holes in our shoes and clothes; most of them were bought at jumble sales. Yet, with Grandad's help, Mam did her best to look after us as best she could, and we never went hungry.

As boys, we were sent regularly to Sunday school, and one memory from that time sticks out above all the rest. When I was seven I had to recite a poem with some other children at the Sunday school meeting at Holy Trinity Church on Down Street. When my turn came to speak, I froze, and felt so terrified that I started to tremble from head to foot; I had never been so scared in my life. From then on, I always avoided anything like that. I became afraid even to speak in class because the other kids could see my shyness. I would blush, lose track of what I was saying and nearly die of embarrassment. This affected my self-confidence throughout my life. I couldn't express myself in front of a group very well because fear always took over. What I wanted to say would often come out wrong. There were times though, that I overdid things, making a spectacle of myself by losing my temper. So it was either one extreme or another – I was either an introvert or an exploding bomb. I guess that not having a dad caused me to build walls of protection around myself, and these were the only ways I knew to handle situations.

Growing up, moving on

It was late 1963 when the local council threw us out of our home, and I was almost 10 years old. I had been playing that day at Poor's Stream where the watercress grew behind Waverly Cricket Park, and returned to find Mam,

four brothers and one sister all waiting for me. I had
nicked some fresh mint from a garden on the way back
down Park Road. I loved mint sauce on any meat. Times
were hard and I felt like I was helping Mam. But there
was no dinner on the table that night. As I entered the
house, I got a clip around the ear.

'Where have you been Brian?' Mam was frantic. 'We've
been waiting for you for over an hour. Get up those stairs
and get washed now! We're going away.'

My sister Susan was not home either but eventually
came in looking as shocked as I was. I hurried upstairs,
confused. My brother John, the eldest, who was fifteen,
followed me and explained:

'We're being kicked out because Grandad owes rent.
You'll all go to a home but I'm not coming with you.'

My jaw dropped.

'I'm going to stay in a friend's house,' he boasted, as if
he had one up on me. But then, looking concerned, he
added softly, 'You'd better not nag Mam, she's very upset,
be a good boy and help her as much as you can.'

I was lost for words for a change and, washing myself
quickly, I hurried downstairs, worried about my mother.
A man from Neath Council was there, urging her to
hurry. A few minutes later, we were on our way to an
unknown destination.

Most of my brothers and sisters had been born in that
house, as had my mother and her brothers and sisters.
This was a very sad day for us all. Everything had to be
left behind – all our family pictures, our furniture and
many other personal possessions. We only took the
clothes that we needed; we never saw our things again.
It seemed like a whole lifetime was being severed from
us, bringing everything we knew and loved to an abrupt
end.

It was times like these that made us all wonder about our fathers. Who and where were they? Mam never talked about it. It was a taboo subject in our family.

We thought also of our Grandma Lillian, who suffered from Alzheimer's disease. What was to become of her? She was very sick and bedridden at that time. (Before her condition got really bad, she would often forget who we were and get mixed up a lot. She would go to the shop to get a pound of sugar and come back with a pound of apples.) Would we ever see her again? We learned later that she had been put in a nursing home, but we heard little else until a couple of years later, when news came that she had died there, alone, without her family near her.

Hector, my grandad, had served in the army during World War II, so how could the company have taken the decision to kick him out of his home of forty-five years when he hit hard times? He had not paid the rent for a few weeks, but it certainly hadn't been more than a month or two. He had to look after Grandma and my mother and her seven children. What a hard world it was – he had paid for that house three times over while working at the Nickel Company. Now, as Grandma went one way, and Mam took us another, he was forced to go away on his own. He managed to find lodgings in Swansea, but he was no longer near us.

Mam was put through a very distressing interview at Neath Council offices. Then we were placed in a homeless families unit in Rhoose, near Cardiff Airport. It was called Rhoose Camp. There were dormitories and a very large hall with tables and benches for each family. The maroon linoleum floor had to be polished daily with buffing machines otherwise Mr Hughes, the master, would get angry. So the floor was always unnervingly shiny and a little slippery, while a strange smell pervaded the whole hall.

It certainly carved the place into my memory. But surprisingly, it wasn't such a terrible time, mainly because we were so close to the airport and the sea. We had a lot of fun watching the planes take off and land and often walked down to the nearby beach to catch crabs and find shells.

We attended Rhoose Primary School and were taunted with jeers from the local children. 'Camp kids! Camp kids!' they shouted. We were picked on for a week or so but the Morris brothers soon made their mark – after all, we had the advantage of numbers. I managed to become the best fighter in the school without fighting. I wrestled with a boy named Callaghan during a gardening lesson and proved myself to be the strongest. He was the second best fighter in the school, and his mate, called Chamberlain, was the best. A couple of days later, there was only one bottle of milk left in the crate and Chamberlain and I went for it. I suggested we share it or fight. He agreed to share it, although he didn't know how scared I was. After that, no one bothered me.

We stayed in Rhoose Camp for six months, until Mam got married to a Mr Ray Jones. After they were wed, the authorities gave them a council house, and we moved back to Clydach to live together. It was only half a mile from where we were born.

Ray had come from up Aberdare way. It wasn't easy for him in those early years of the sixties. We were not the best-behaved young boys and sometimes I got into trouble with the police for petty crime. Ray took on the challenge of looking after an instant family, and a large one at that. It wasn't easy for him – our rebellious natures frequently caused rows between him and Mam. He worked very hard as a gas supply installer, often working late because of gas leaks. He was short and stocky, with huge thick-fingered hands that had become very rough and hard. He was one of the hardest working men I ever knew, out in all weathers.

Soon the red-headed twins Carl and Christina were born. Now, with Ray and Mam included, there were eleven of us. She never stopped cooking, cleaning, washing clothes, ironing, and raising us all.

It was at this time that I made my first of many court appearances, which only added to the stress of a busy household. I was charged with stealing the contents of a chocolate machine that hung on the wall outside the local newsagents and with breaking into the house of a man while playing truant from school one afternoon. Then, four or five of us 12-year-old boys were caught ransacking a classmate's house while he and his parents were away for a few days. They were all regarded as minor offences, but I did come pretty close to being sent to Borstal.

I left school as soon as I could in the summer of 1969, about six months after my fifteenth birthday (the school leaving age back then). I got my first job as a potato sorter and deliverer on Ward's Farm in Alltwen, three miles from home.

'That's a fine chipper,' old Mr Ward would say, admiring his King Edwards.

After sorting out the good spuds from the blighted ones, we packed and delivered them to chip shops around Glamorgan. I loved going with Mr Ward's son Roy to farms in Pembrokeshire and Herefordshire to fetch a load of spuds on the potato farms. It was great because I didn't have to work while enjoying the ride. My hair grew long and the sun bleached it a golden blonde. It was a great time to be sixteen.

A group of us young 'hippies' started to smoke grass and hashish and listened to music by Jimi Hendrix, Bob

Dylan and Pink Floyd. Drugs and music were suddenly the only things that seemed to matter. The only time you wouldn't find us sitting smoking to records was on Thursday nights – and that was because we were in the TV room of the local Public Hall, watching *Top of the Pops*. I bought my first guitar – a Hofner Compensator – for £7 off a mate and soon became known by the boys as the 'one string wonder'. My ability to follow and copy, note for note, guitar solos from albums while they played was quite remarkable. Roy Harper; Crosby, Stills, Nash, and Young; and many others. All on one string!

It was here that I first met Kerry Jenkins, a man who would later play a very important part in my life. He was superintendent for road maintenance in the area, and a lay preacher in his spare time. He'd also lived in the same street as my family. He was able to give me my next job as labourer on a tarmac gang, where we patched up roads in the Swansea and Neath valleys. He used to come into the park where we smoked grass and hashish and tell us that Jesus loved us. We used to snigger about it, but he was a great character, so we didn't mind having him around. When some of us moved into commune-style living (that is, ten or so of us renting big houses together), Kerry often came and listened to our discussions about life, death, the 'astral plain' and other dimensions. His reasoning and arguments about the Bible sank in a bit, but we thought we had advanced from that old 'religious' stuff and knew better. Those were philosophical and experimental times for us young 'far out' hippies.

London

Back at home, Ray and Mam were arguing a lot because of our behaviour and his drink problem. So when I was sixteen I escaped to London, following my brother Raymond who had already been there for two years. I didn't realise that my sisters would miss me so much – Susan used to write through tears to tell me all the news from Clydach.

That was just after Jimi Hendrix died in September 1970. He had choked on his own vomit after taking a combination of pills and alcohol. Just one month earlier, four of us had travelled to the third Isle of Wight Pop Festival in my brother John's Morris 1000 car and watched him play live. I loved this brilliant, shy guitarist and was heavily influenced by and looked up to him at the time. His music had been inspired partly by LSD, but mostly by his hard life. He was wild and beautiful – no one could play like him, and even to this day no-one has again.

I went to many other pop festivals during those early hippie years. One of the first and best was in the city of Bath, next to the river, when one of the smaller acts was a little-known British group called Led Zeppelin. A year later they topped the bill in Shepton Mallet, at what they called the Bath Contemporary Rhythm & Blues Festival, which was the forerunner of the Glastonbury Festival. We called ourselves 'freaks' and believed we were cool and 'happening'.

In London, most of the work I did was on building sites or the occasional cleaning job. I didn't want to go home even when times were tough. It was an achievement to have lasted a year. I went to rock gigs at the Greyhound pub on Fulham Palace Road on Fridays and Saturdays, and many of the bands I saw became very big later on. I didn't want to fail and, although the cash often ran out, I managed to stick at it for a year. Eventually though, the money, the jobs and the reasons to stay there really did run out. The bright lights dimmed a bit, and, still just a seventeen-year-old, I got homesick and made my way back to Wales.

London hadn't just been about music though. I'd taken a significant step forward in one of my other interests while I was there: I'd tried my first LSD tab in Wardour Street in the West End. I came back to Wales thinking I was all hip and cool, and brought with me fifty Californian Sunshine LSD tabs to sell. This was my first attempt at dealing drugs. I sold one or two but, even though I could have sold many more, I ended up sharing them with all the hippies of the valley.

It was just after this that I got my first drugs charge from the police. I was caught with 96 milligrams of cannabis sativa (grass) – not even enough for a tiny cigarette joint. I got fined £75, which would equate to about £750 today. It took me a year to pay it all off and I worked hard to do it. Kerry Jenkins helped me out by giving me back my old job as a tarmac spreader, and although it was hard work, I managed to make the best of it. At least I got a tan working outdoors – I was a right poser standing on the back of our lorry with my long sun-streaked hair blowing in the wind.

Back to Clydach

Settled again in Wales, I started to take more drugs and party harder than ever before. We saw a lot of the police, a lot of the opposite sex and, thanks to the LSD, a lot of things that weren't really there. We thought we were so cool.

One night we had an LSD party over at 'The Kingdom', a place where most Clydach boys and girls went for some time alone. I don't know where the name came from – it had been passed down from older generations – but whenever it was mentioned, it was always synonymous with sex. It was an area of wasteland across the 'green bridge' on the River Tawe in Clydach, and it was where most of us lost our virginity.

There must have been about thirty to forty of us having a whale of a time, singing and making a racket all night long. Gazing up at the stars was an awesome sight when we were tripping – everything looks so different when you're high on that stuff. We lit a big fire and just sat there all night – some of us strumming on guitars, others drumming away with sticks on tins.

'Police!' shouted someone suddenly.

There was a slight panic, but it didn't last long. We all realised we had no drugs in our pockets, and we relaxed. All the drugs we'd had were now safely inside us, and they couldn't bust us for those.

The police dogs seemed to know that we'd been up to something though – they were barking fiercely and scared us back out of relaxation. To us, fuelled by all these drugs, they appeared like snarling monsters, with huge dripping white fangs and demonic red eyes.

It was a major operation with about twenty or thirty officers involved. No arrests were made – we were simply told to go home. Some did but many of us went to Kerry Jenkins' house to talk about what we had experienced. We thought we'd had some kind of religious experience that night, and he seemed like the best person to talk to in those circumstances.

Another time, a well-known drug squad detective called Basil approached us when we were sitting on a park bench, and asked us if we knew about any drugs in the valley. This was a bit like asking the local butcher if he knew of any meat, but poor Basil didn't know about my previous drugs conviction. We put on our dumbest-sounding welsh accents and lied: 'We never see drugs in Clydach see.' We laughed our heads off when he'd gone. We'd been tripping on LSD all along.

Back to London

Not long after, some of us moved to London again. It was 1973, and I'd begun to come of age. I was starting to take a very keen interest in the ladies, and as soon as I was back in the capital I went to visit Maria, a beautiful girl with long black hair and lovely brown eyes that I had met in Cornwall on holiday. She lived in the basement of the Austrian Embassy in Belgravia Mews, because her parents were caretakers there.

Our relationship developed, and before too long Maria became pregnant. I offered to do the right thing and marry her, but we were not in love. She declined my offer, saying that it would not work out, and so we went our separate ways. Little Erika was born at King's Cross Hospital on the 6th November 1973. I held her in my arms for barely a moment – but in that moment, as I gazed down at this miraculous, beautiful little person, I felt a wave of emotion that was stronger than any drug. It seems strange to speak of being a father so quickly, but the truth is I only saw her once more after that, on her first birthday. I gave her a little teddy bear. I often wonder what became of her, and whether she kept hold of my gift.

I found a squat in Pimlico near Victoria Station, and moved in there with some Welsh friends. One day while we were walking through the station we spotted these two stunning girls: Eugenie, who was Indonesian, and

Eleonora, her half-Dutch, half-Indonesian cousin. They came over to us and asked if we knew where they could stay cheaply.

'Yes!' I suggested hopefully. 'You can stay with us in our beautiful squat!'

They giggled together excitedly and answered 'Yes, thanks,' in unison. I could not believe our luck.

I was smitten and fell in love with Eleonora (Noor for short) from the start. We were both nineteen. She had very long red hair, which contrasted beautifully with my long blonde locks; together we looked a picture. Her mixed blood made her look striking – men would turn and look at her wherever she went. We spent most of the time together – I was chuffed as could be!

But just two months later, it was time for them to go back to Holland (as their Interail tickets were expiring). We spluttered our tearful goodbyes at the station and I wondered whether I would ever see her again.

For the next few days and weeks I could not get her out of my mind. I'd fallen deeper in love than I'd realised. Every waking moment I had, I kept thinking about jumping on a boat and going over to Holland to look for her. And then, somewhere along the line, I stopped just thinking about it and decided to do something ridiculous . . . .

THREE

Travelling with Noor

Three months later I was setting out for Holland, determined to find my wonderful new girlfriend, Noor. She was lovely, so different; I was intrigued by that unusual and eye-catching face of hers and just had to see it again. I turned up at the address I had for her in The Hague in search of her, only to be told by the neighbours that Noor and Eugenie were not home. But after waiting an hour, they arrived home from work together on their bicycles. There I was, sitting on their steps, filling Noor with amazement. She had thought, naturally I suppose, that she would never see me again and after a while had all but got over me. Now there were tears of joy in her eyes. We hugged and kissed each other, and our love for one another came flooding back.

It was great to be in Holland. Everything was new and an adventure for me. I loved the easy-going Dutch and, pretty obviously, I loved their relaxed attitude to drugs. Almost everyone enjoyed speaking English – so there was no problem with communication — and there was no pressure on me to learn the language.

Eugenie had a German-American boyfriend named Yves and he asked us if we would like to stay on his friend's farm in Germany. We jumped at the chance and had the perfect summer in the beautiful Bavarian countryside helping out with the harvest of maize. A barn served as our accommodation and I started to feel like a real cosmopolitan living in all these different countries.

However, two months later and almost into autumn, the money ran out (a familiar phrase for me at this time) and I had to return home to Wales. Noor wanted to come with me, and she decided to work in Wales for a year. Not long after she arrived, she found a job in Morriston hospital as a cleaner, but she hated it. She couldn't get along with the other women there.

Noor often had dark moods and would get very jealous if I even glanced at another woman – even if I simply made a comment about one on the television. It was really hard sometimes to help her to snap out of the moods. She had an innocent and wonderful child-like idea of love, and I tried to give her all the attention that I could. I massaged her when she had back pains and used to comb her long red hair because it became easily tangled after sleep. I tried my best when I was out with her not to talk to anyone else's girlfriend, however innocently, because otherwise when we got back home she wouldn't talk to me for days. I don't deny I had an eye for the ladies but I was faithful to her. I just couldn't be the perfect picture of love that she wanted.

We shared a flat with my brother David and our friend Chris near Morriston, about two miles from Clydach. One time Noor and I travelled to a pop festival in Bickershaw, near Liverpool, and after two days returned home exhausted at six in the morning. We went straight to bed, just as David and Chris were leaving for work. Then, at about 7.30 a.m., there was a knock at the door.

'Social security!' someone shouted through the letterbox.

I'd not slept for two days, and wasn't particularly interested in seeing anyone – especially not social security. But I yawned and opened the door.

It wasn't social security. Instead, plain-clothes detectives burst in like they were busting terrorists. Some headed straight to the back door to let in others who had covered the back of the building. Each room was searched and thoroughly turned upside down. I felt rather self-satisfied, knowing that we didn't have any drugs there, and showed them confidently around each room. When we got to the room which Chris and David shared, one detective asked if I had access to their room.

'Yes, we all share the flat together,' was the wrong thing to say, in hindsight.

That cost me a £100 fine after they found a small amount of cannabis resin (hashish) and some grass in a coat pocket and a drawer. It was enough for two cigarette joints. In court I pleaded that nothing had been found in our room, but it was to no avail. I certainly didn't have access to their belongings – that's how, as I said earlier, evidence can be twisted to go against you.

I was fined £100 – more than Chris or David because it was my second drugs bust. £100 was a lot of money in those days. Fortunately, I was working for the Gas Board and could pay the fine this time, in about three months. But after that ugly experience, the desire to leave Wales once and for all was growing in us both.

Life in Holland

We left for Holland in April of the following year, 1975. We stayed with Noor's parents, Hugo and Toos, for a few weeks until Hugo found an attic flat for us. He also got me a job as an animal caretaker in a research centre near Delft. I cleaned the boxes of rats and mice before being 'promoted' to working with rhesus monkeys.

Hermon the foreman wanted me to learn Dutch, so he stopped speaking English. It took quite a while, but Hermon was patient and persevered with me. It took two years before I was able to have a confident conversation in Dutch – I found it an exceptionally hard language to learn. I stayed in that job for three years, eventually leaving because of the growing feeling against animal testing. I couldn't handle all the frowns and comments I received when I told people where I was working.

After that I took various jobs on building sites as a labourer and had one short spell in a milk factory. We worked, smoked hashish and grass and went to the Paard van Troje (Horse of Troy) regularly to see bands. Soft drugs were openly sold there. It was probably the first place in The Hague where they were sold legally. I became increasingly paranoid from the effects of smoking dope but I found it too hard to say no when I was offered some of the stuff.

We both continued to save money from working hard. Our love for travel meant that we spent most of what we had on Interail tickets, and so although we never had much money, we got to see most of Europe.

Our relationship was up and down. Although I was faithful, Noor still didn't trust me and, even if I simply expressed interest in what a woman said, she became moody and depressed again. When pressed about it later she would burst into tears and say that I never spoke to her as nicely.

We just seemed to grow apart over the years. Then, in January 1979, Noor came home from office work at the state printers and told me she had fallen for a married man there. I was devastated! We had been together for about six years – for most of the 1970s. For the next couple of weeks we spent most of our time trying to talk it through, with little sleep in between. She smoked hash practically non-stop and I'm sure now, in hindsight, that it was helping her to become increasingly confused. I couldn't handle the stuff: the paranoia eventually caused me to stop smoking it because I became too self-conscious. Anyway, due to a mixture of her drugs and her evaporating feelings for me, Noor eventually left to stay with her parents.

Despite my unhappiness I managed to find work in the midst of winter. Getting a new job during that crisis was a bonus because it helped me concentrate on my life and not mope about. I was a labourer in the Huis Ten Bosch (House of the Woods), which was one of Queen Juliana's palaces in The Hague. It was being renovated for Beatrix, the Queen's daughter, who was to become Queen two years later. I often saw them both around the site while I was working. Some of Rembrandt's largest paintings hung in the Oranje Zaal (Hall of Orange) and I went there to have a sneaky look. The famous 'Night Watch' was housed there, and I saw it with my own eyes (well, it may have been a copy, but I'll always believe it was the real thing). It was great to be working for this reputable company which specialised in renovating historic buildings.

For two years, I worked hard on the job before I got bored again. When I decided to leave, I did so only after making a pact with myself that I would learn a genuine trade. I was tired of hopping from bottom-rung job to bottom-rung job, and applied for a government-training course as a carpenter. My application was successful and it wasn't long before I was happily occupied with the course. I progressed from making stools and boxes to cupboards with sliding doors, then moved on to putting up windows, doors, roofs, floors and stairs.

One day I had an accident while cutting some wood. My mind was not on the job; I was miles away, thinking about Noor. Sleep had escaped me yet again the night before. I blinked repeatedly as I pushed almost a complete table leg through the circular saw. I couldn't get her out of my head. The whirring sound of the spinning blade cutting through oak was fading as my mind drifted off. . . .

I must be crazy, I thought. Why can't I let go? I'm only 27 – I've got my whole life ahead of me. Why am I even learning to become a carpenter when I've never had the slightest interest before?

The sound of a screeching, straining blade brought me back to reality. There was a loud thud and searing pain in my hand. The teeth of the saw had struck a notch halfway down the table leg. Half-asleep, I had loosened my grip on the leg and, as the metal had hit the notch, the wood had slammed into the palm of my hand. The instructor, Mr Jansen, was already on the scene switching off the machine. My hand was cut and I cursed in shock.

'Stupid machine!' I yelled. 'Look what's happened now. That's it! I'm not even interested in being a carpenter, and one day I'm going to end up losing a hand! I'm sorry Mr Jansen, I'll never become a carpenter, and I'm too clumsy. It's just not me working on a machine that could kill me. I'm going home after lunch.'

I started to turn pale and felt like throwing up. I put my head between my knees to let the blood flow back. I was in shock.

Later, after receiving four stitches, I sat with Jan, one of the other trainees, for lunch. He was six-foot-two, blonde haired: a man with the typical Dutch look. We got on well because we shared a love of travel – Jan had travelled to India and Sri Lanka a few months before. Normally we'd sit and talk about different countries we'd been to, but this time, because of the accident, I began to tell him how I had been feeling. I just started talking, and everything poured out.

I told him how recently I had seen Noor walking the streets in a daze. She had suffered a nervous breakdown just after leaving me and had hacked off all her hair in a couple of mad minutes. Nothing had come of her short-lived relationship with the married man, and she had begun to hear voices in her head. Her parents had to have her admitted to a psychiatric unit, where she was diagnosed with schizophrenia and manic depression. They let her out after two months but she was re-admitted time after time. Her condition did not improve, and the strong antidepressants they gave her only made her worse. It was very painful to see her now on the street looking dirty, talking to herself loudly and laughing at the sky. I could do nothing. If I approached her, she would behave even more wildly. I would go to her parent's house to see if I could help in any way. I had even been searching the streets, afraid that someone there would hurt her.

Jan listened as I poured out my heart.

'Ever since she left me eighteen months ago, Jan, I can't sleep,' I continued. 'I can't concentrate, I drink too much and I've even started writing broken heart poems! I'm losing it and I need a break. Somewhere far away; somewhere nice and relaxed; somewhere different. Any ideas?'

'Sri Lanka is very far away, and completely different,' suggested Jan.

Geography was one of my favourite subjects at school – a subject I would sometimes come top of the class in. We had studied the beautiful country of Sri Lanka, which in my schooldays was known as Ceylon. Pictures of colourfully dressed women picking tea on the plantations were etched on my memory.

'It's a tropical island with golden beaches, and high mountains, and it's covered with coconuts and tea,' Jan informed me. He had stayed there for two months.

'It's a British colony isn't it?' I asked.

'Not any more. They got independence in 1948, but you can still see the British, Dutch and Portuguese influence all around the island, and you know Brian, I stayed with fishermen and managed on £2 a day. And half of that was spent on booze and fags.' He laughed. I was amazed.

'Wow! £2 a day with the comforts of life as well. I'm off to Sri Lanka!' I was grinning, certain that I was going.

'Why don't you start saving now and go as soon as possible Brian? It will do you the world of good; I think you will get on well with the people there.'

'Yes,' was all I could reply before my mind drifted to tropical beaches and tea plantations on a beautiful island far away. This would be an excellent way to put the sadness of recent months firmly in the past. I thanked Jan and left for home, mesmerised by dreams of adventure.

FOUR

Sri Lankan dawn

It didn't take me long to propel myself into action once my mind was set. I sold a lot of my valuables and cashed in some saving stamps. I found a friend to look after my flat – he needed a place to stay and gave me a nice deposit. So within in a few weeks I had got enough to go. I'd decided that 3,000 guilders (about £1,200 then) would be plenty, as that would be enough for a ticket and spending money. I left the training centre, and bought the cheapest one-year open ticket I could find with Kuwait Airways. And as that ticket landed in my palm, in the late autumn of 1981, things moved almost effortlessly from impulsive idea to unlikely reality.

The day of my departure, the 27th November, finally arrived. I sat on the fast train to Amsterdam's Schiphol Airport reading a guidebook I had bought. I felt on top of the world – the anticipation of my first long-haul flight was giving me an excitement I had never felt before. The East had always intrigued me, and now I was actually going there, to a culture and environment that was certain to be like nothing I'd ever seen or experienced. I walked into the airport with a spring in my step, then, having sunk a few quick pints at the bar, headed for the departure gate tipsy and beaming. I managed to find my way onto the right plane, and despite spotting a couple of stunning stewardesses I thought better of making a fool of myself. Instead I just sat back as my journey roared into life, and enjoyed the wonderful feeling of hope that this new start was providing.

One memory from that flight will stay with me forever, like a great framed picture hanging inside my head. It was when we flew over the beautiful Maldive Islands. They looked like sparkling pearls surrounded by multi-coloured reefs in a turquoise sea. It was the most stunning sight I had ever seen, and only further buoyed my mood.

No more than an hour after that moment of marvel, I watched Sri Lanka loom into view, fringed by white beaches and covered densely with palm trees. My excitement grew still further as we approached our final destination. We descended through thick monsoon clouds to touch down at the airport near Colombo. As our eleven-hour journey finally came to an end, I couldn't wait for the doors to open. But when they did, it was like walking into a greenhouse! The humidity was overwhelming – it was clear immediately that this would take some getting used to. The air-conditioned Arrivals buildings brought relief, but only for about half an hour.

There were many hustling touts about trying to get me into their taxis and hotels. Throngs of people surrounded me on the hot street outside the airport, but I was determined not to give in. I knew that I had to stretch my money in order to be able to stay as long as possible, so I headed for the bus to Colombo with a trail of people chasing me. I was the only Westerner going for the bus.

'Sir, sir! Come come, you come my taxi, very cheap, very cheap!' pleaded the most persistent of them.

'No, no!' I asserted, hoping he and his colleagues would leave me alone. 'I'm catching the bus, I'm not a rich man.'

Yet, I suppose I had more money in my pocket than any of these poor people would see in a year. The taxi was 400 rupees for the twenty-two-mile journey, which was about £8. The bus was only 14 rupees, and I knew that I needed to be disciplined.

I was already sweating heavily thanks to my heavy rucksack, but getting onto the smoke-filled Ceylon Transport Board bus was another experience altogether. It was so crowded that I literally couldn't move my arms or legs, and by the time I got to Colombo I was soaking from head to toe. I squelched off of the bus at Bristol Street – where the guidebook told me that the Ex-Servicemen's club and a YMCA were, and where cheap rooms were available. As I walked along the road, child beggars were pulling at my shirt pleading for a little of my money. There were other beggars with limbs missing sitting on the street corners. One particular man I noticed sitting on a low wooden board with ball-bearing wheels, pulling his legless body along with his arms. People with limbs that had swollen huge from elephantiasis and leprosy were lying on the pavement, also begging. My first experience of poverty on this scale was an eye-opener and culture shock indeed.

It was only a short walk to where I was going and I was relieved to get myself off the busy street. I checked in at the desk of the Ex-Servicemen's Club, where pictures of Queen Elizabeth II, Prince Philip and Lord Mountbatten hung (they made me feel much more at home). For a pound, I was given a simple, clean room with a fan. Having spent the last few hours close to melting point, the ability to now take a cold shower, then lie on the bed with the overhead fan on full-blast gave a feeling of relief which is practically indescribable. Finally, after a prolonged period with the fan, I felt cool enough to dress.

I didn't want to suffer from the time lag, so I was determined not to sleep until night. I needed to keep drinking to stay awake, so made my way toward the bar and sat there, waiting for it to open. It was still only 10 a.m. though, so I went outside and bought a copy of the Ceylon Daily News to read while I was waiting. The bar soon opened and I bought a large bottle of Lion Lager and settled down to read. In no time, the tables around me filled up with Colombo's white-collar workers.

Two men asked if they could sit at my table, and I was pleased for the chance to talk. One of them was Pattu, who was about 50 years old, very thin, with a little pointed goatee beard. He worked as the Deputy Chief Engineer for the Colombo Port Authority. With him was Peter, who was about 40. A larger, rounder man with a wonderful belly laugh, he was a businessman who imported aluminium. Both spoke English and Sinhalese intermittently.

Pattu introduced us and ordered a bottle of Coconut Arrack, which is a strong but smooth liquor made from the coconut palm. It didn't taste anything like coconuts but went down well. After a few minutes of conversation Peter ordered some 'bites'. This was a plate of whatever was on offer that day: sometimes it was dried fish or fried potato chips or even peanuts. Whatever the 'bites' happened to be on a given day, the contents of the plate would always be laced with very hot chillies that increased the thirst.

Peter, whose accent almost sounded welsh, told me he was a descendant of the Dutch Burghers (Eurasians) and that there was a rich mixture of cultures on the island, mainly due to the many times that it had changed imperial hands. We were all getting rather drunk. I wanted to go outside for a walk but Peter told me that it was not a good idea to be on my own in Colombo on my first day.

'There are too many rogues in Colombo, Brian. You will lose everything! I can't allow you to walk around this part of Colombo. Please come home with me. It's my pleasure indeed to have you visit my place!'

I couldn't get a word in but thought it was a good idea and thanked him. Peter let out an elated 'Hare hare!' (Meaning 'OK!'), and moved his head in a strange-looking way. This, I later discovered, is the common Sri Lankan head waggle: not a nod, nor a shake, but something in between.

Peter's home was about eighteen miles from Colombo on the Kandy Road. His wife Irene, her two daughters and Peter's visiting brothers made me feel so welcome. The hospitality was wonderful; the food was superb. Outside, their garden was full of wildlife. Huge, noisy (and thankfully harmless) flying insects in metallic greens and blacks; the sounds and sights of colourful tropical birds; the large and little lizards skittering through dead leaves. These were everyday sights, like the sparrows and starlings that were ten-a-penny at home. After a week, my interest having been further aroused by these strange spectacles, I got restless and wanted to explore more of the island, so Peter took me with him to visit his mother in the South.

I was entranced by the many paradisiacal beaches that lay along the coast road. There were Buddhist temples there, palms which hung over shimmering blue seas and lagoons, and picturesque hardwood catamarans bobbing on the ocean. I stopped a while to gaze at the latter, as fishermen balanced on their thin craft with simple bamboo rods in their hands. Their sarongs were tucked high up their thighs, while the straw hats on their heads gave them the only shade in the blazing heat. Every few minutes, as we progressed steadily along the road, Ceylon Transport Board buses, private minibuses and lorries, all chock-a-block full, sped past to and from Colombo. Bullocks pulling heavy-laden carts swayed precariously, almost toppling over as they hugged the curb to let the vehicles pass. Flea-ridden dogs with most of their coat scratched away lazily snoozed in the middle of the road, getting out of the way just in time as each vehicle approached. Giant stone statues of the Buddha were everywhere I looked. I found it hard to take in all the unfamiliar sights and sounds. I didn't want to blink for fear of missing something.

A special guest

After a four-hour drive, we arrived at Peter's family home: a big colonial country house set among banana, rice and coconut plantations. I was introduced to Peter's mother, sister, brothers, and servants, and made to feel very special and welcome. The servants giggled as I discarded my knife and fork, using my right hand to enjoy the rice and curry. I gave them a head waggle; smiled and jested, 'hare rasai!' (very tasty). I told everyone I was a carpenter, although I had only completed a one-year course. Everyone laughed again as I learned to say 'Mama waduwa' (I am a carpenter). I had picked up a few words from my guidebook and this seemed to impress them. It was so good to be treated as a special guest in this lovely setting. The arrack went down well and I gained a wonderful impression of Sri Lanka's hospitality.

A family friend named Gamini arrived on a moped. He was eager to show me a very special beach adjacent to a fishing village about eight miles away. Part of me – the adventurous spirit that had got me this far I guess – wanted to go right then, but I was very tired and my head spun from the booze. I had seen enough for one day: anything more would have to wait until tomorrow. In keeping with the rest of the hospitality, I was given my own room with a fan and had a very comfortable night.

The next morning, after water pumped straight from the family well had provided me with a uniquely refreshing shower, Gamini took me to that beautiful beach. As soon as I set eyes on the place, called Unawatuna, I fell in love with it, and knew that I wanted to stay. The beach curved inland in a huge semi-circle that stretched for about two and a half miles, and a brilliantly white Buddhist temple sat at one end amid overhanging palms. A reef protected the golden sands, and the water on the beach side was calm and fantastic for snorkelling. Hand carved heavy wood catamarans lined this peaceful fishing village, but tourism was bringing change even here. A few restaurants had sprung up along the bay and I was able to get a room for 20 rupees a day with a poor fisherman's family.

The next day I met and befriended a man name Chandra in his peaceful little restaurant at the end of the beach near the temple. He was sitting at one of the tables, with his long black beard and a red spot on his forehead, pretending to be some kind of wise guru. I teased him that he was a 'boru' (false) guru. He laughed loudly but asked me not to let on because I could spoil his business.

It was here that I also met Samson. He was small and wiry, and strong too, though he didn't look like a mighty man. A fisherman who had fallen on hard times, he was glad to work there waiting tables in order to feed his family. Years of hard rowing four or five miles out to sea everyday were evident on his weather-worn, sun-scorched skin. He was able to talk to me in pidgin English. I sat and enjoyed our conversation watching the waves lap at the shore barely ten yards away.

The Rolling Stones were playing on Chandra's radio cassette recorder, which he powered with an old car battery. Occasionally, shoals of small fish dived out of the water to escape the hungry tuna that had given them chase. The sound amazed me. It was like thousands of stones raining down, splashing against the surface.

'You like-a come look-a my house Mr Brian?' asked Samson, as I sat there, enchanted by this tropical paradise.

'Yes, I'd like that.'

There was something about Samson that drew me to him. He had a great smile and laugh, and his poverty gave him an honesty that I admired and identified with. His little house, the roof of which had been damaged by the recent monsoon rains, was near some huge rocks reached through a hundred yards of thick jungle. Rhesus macaque monkeys squabbled in the trees above. I recognised them because of my job in the research centre six years before in Holland. Papaya, mango, jak fruit and banana grew all around. Also in the trees were parakeets and many other very colourful exotic birds of paradise. I was able to identify some of them from pictures in the guidebook.

Samson's wife Wimala and her seven children stared wide-eyed in amazement at their 'suddha' (white) guest. Their broad smiles flashed gleaming white teeth. I almost melted with humble gratitude for their warm acceptance of me. I was delighted when they asked me to stay. The 50 rupees (90p) a day that I gave them was, incredibly, enough to feed the whole family and myself. I washed daily at the local public well and always enjoyed speaking with the people there. I always spoke the Sinhalese words that I had learned and was able to add daily to my vocabulary because everyone wanted to teach me. It was a wonderful way for me to learn about the Sri Lankan culture and language. Samson's Buddhist family taught me Sinhalese and I taught them English, all in a very simple way. I loved Samson for his honesty and character, his wife Wimala's excellent Sri Lankan cooking, and the children's bright smiles and obvious delight at having me there. Samson and I went everywhere together and became inseparable.

India

Time moved on. After three months, my visa ran out and I had to leave the country. I decided to go to South India for a month and then return, as the visa could then be reissued on entry. I travelled north to Talaimannar to cross on the newly re-opened ferry to Rameswaram in Tamil Nadu State. This route closed again soon afterwards because the Tamil Tigers of Jaffna and the northeast of the Island had begun their campaign for a separate state, so I was very lucky to experience a journey that very few tourists have made.

The boat was jam-packed with Tamil traders on their way to buy Indian cloth that they could sell in Sri Lanka for a generous profit. It was a beautiful day and the sparkling sea was calm. The warm tropical air blew gently against my face as I looked expectantly towards India. I could make out colourful pyramids reaching above the sea, which turned out to be structures on the fronts of Hindu temples. Their elaborately carved walls became clearer as we approached: colourfully-painted figures from Hindu culture crowded the walls. Mythical creatures, animals and human forms all seemed to be fighting for space – a symbol that this was deepest traditional Hindu India.

I found a very cheap 'lodge' in the town and asked for a room with a shower. The tiny old man who worked there – thin, grey and bespectacled he was – showed me the smallest room I had ever seen and offered it to me for 10 rupees. It was only five feet by seven feet. Ten feet from the door was a well with a rope and bucket, enclosed by a wall. I didn't mind at all and found it great fun, after all, I had already been washing in a well in Unawatuna for quite a while. Later I walked to the temple, which was full of orange-robed saddhus (holy men) and devotees covered in coloured powder. They were laying flowers at the feet of imposing statues. Ganesh had the body of a human with an elephant's face and Shiva stood in a circle with six arms, brightly painted in many colours. A procession of camels, elephants and white cows were paraded through the temple. Men blew on long thin horns, while others beat endlessly on drums that hung on their shoulders. Fire torches were held aloft and swung around in the hands of dancers dressed in beautiful costumes. Thousands of candles flickered, and devotees continually added more with each offering. It was all so mesmerising that I became very tired. I returned to my shoebox room, knowing that I needed to leave the next morning for Kerala State.

First of all, crossing Tamil Nadu State in a week was a learning experience that shocked, surprised and amazed me. I had never imagined such a vast and diverse India. The contrast of poverty and the splendour of the big city villas and hotels separating poor and rich were ever present and ever thought-provoking. There were marvellous temples, multi-coloured vehicles adorned with mirrors and trinkets, and elephants dragging huge logs. Pungent odours of spices and incense, free roaming 'holy' white cows with huge horns munching away on refuse at the roadside, and ten kinds of monkey on streets and shoulders. The place is simply unforgettable.

When I reached the Kerala coast on the Indian Ocean, I stayed at Kovalam, a very popular place for backpackers to relax on the beach for a couple of weeks. After that, I travelled on by ferry through lagoons, canals and backwaters to Alleppy. Here I wanted to buy some of the powerful local cannabis grass, one of the 'best' cannabis strains in the world. It wasn't long before a willing man took me to a farm nearby where I bought a half a kilo of the stuff for about $100 (which was way overpriced – but I was hardly on familiar enough territory here to argue). I planned to take it back to Sri Lanka to sell, enabling me to extend my holiday there. It had been a while since I'd dealt drugs, but it was the one sure-fire way I knew to make lots of money, and so I returned to the pursuit quite willingly.

I noticed that the man who acted as my guide had followed me back to my lodge. I played it friendly with him and let him come inside with me, but I didn't trust him. Eventually, when he left my room, I decided that it would not be a good idea to stay. I was afraid he might return with the police, so I slipped out of the back door and left town on the overnight bus to Madurai. Then I started to wonder how I would bring the dope back to Sri Lanka on the ferry. The next morning, after I had checked into a lodge, I went out and bought two Thermos flasks: one small and one large. Back in my room I took out the delicate inner glass flasks and switched them so that the small glass container went into the large outer covering. I packed the grass tightly in the space between. I was quite pleased with myself and decided it was time to take the train back to Rameswaram for the ferry.

I had wanted to fill the flask with hot tea or coffee but going through customs, I realised that I'd forgotten all about it. I could only see a 'Milk Bar' right next to the customs gate, so I hurried across and bought some chocolate milk, as there was nothing else for sale. Pouring the thick liquid into the flask I smiled at the bemused onlookers, offering only, 'keeps nice and cool for the ferry!' There was no problem with customs. Once on board I went to the toilet to check it, and got a nasty shock. The glass had broken and the grass had soaked up all the liquid, making for a gooey, soggy mess! There was no way I could hide it now if the Sri Lanka customs opened the flask.

I was determined to succeed after coming this far; and rather than throw the whole thing overboard, I decided to go for it. As I approached the customs gate my heart started to beat very fast and a few beads of sweat began to trickle down my face. Yet there were no problems at Talaimannar. There were only about four Westerners, and we were waved through like special guests, while the hundreds of Sri Lankans and Indians all carrying bags crammed with Indian cloth waited a long time to be cleared. I grinned to myself as I walked onto the bus, then reflected with a gulp on what fate might have befallen me had I been caught.

After a rough six hours, but a very cheap £1 minibus ride to Colombo, I checked into the YMCA in Bristol Street, next door to the Ex-Servicemen's Club where I had stayed before. I opened the flask and wondered whether the contents were salvageable. I picked out the glass pieces and squeezed as much of the thick sticky milk out as I could, tipping it away. Drinking it would have spaced me right out! Spreading the grass out on newspaper, I switched on the fan, and went out to a bar. When I got back, it was completely dry. It had a slightly strange smell but, apart from that it was OK. I stayed in my room after I tried it and was right out of my mind. It was the only grass I had smoked for a few years, and once was definitely enough. It made me paranoid, and I kept on checking the corridor and looking out of the window for any cops.

I finally arrived back in Unawatuna and got down to selling the grass as quickly as I could to a tourist dealer. I made about $600 profit on it, which was enough to let me stay very comfortably for another month. I paid for a new roof for Samson's house, and a bed as well. It was wonderful to be welcomed back by the family again. I often enjoyed playing with the children in the warm tropical water. I loved the sea so much that I thought nothing of swimming out to the rock a mile offshore, taking a snorkel and mask. Sometimes I spotted two-metre-long hammerhead sharks swimming under me. I would freak and say a quick prayer. I don't know why I kept praying, obviously it was something that had stayed with me from my childhood.

One day on the beach I met Jay, an Englishman who lived in California. Knowing I was leaving for Holland in a week, he asked if he could stop off at my flat with some hashish about a month later. What a good earner that would be, I thought. Life was becoming easy. I liked it!

The sun-soaked Island of Ceylon has been a stop-over for thousands of years for travellers. The wide smiles and wide-armed hospitality of its people draws you magnetically to its tranquil shores, and the place is blessed with such idyllic beauty that, as I learned, it's very hard to leave. No wonder the sailor traders of old gave the place the Arab name of Serendib (from which the word 'serene' is derived).

But after five months, the time to say goodbye finally arrived. Samson brought me to the airport in a neighbour's taxi, and tears were in both of our eyes as we regretfully said our goodbyes. Back in the air again a couple of hours later, I looked down from the plane at that sandy coastline. In that moment I suddenly realised that this trip had been a complete success – I had seen a new and exciting place, and met new people, but more importantly I was finally over the disappointment of losing Noor. Without warning, tears of happiness flooded my eyes and I whispered another unplanned prayer: 'Thank you God for making all this possible. You have been so good to me.'

FIVE

Tailed by the dragon

Back in The Hague, I met a man named Joshua who sold cocaine. He was a very tall Dutch man of about my age, and he lived very close to a bar called the Ned Kelly Café where I used to drink. He and I would often go back to his flat together, where we snorted through the night talking about everything and nothing, and repeating ourselves over and over without realising it. He told me that in his life, friends have come and gone, and that most were only ever after his coke. I told him that I was different, but he replied cynically that 'they all say that'. In fact, Joshua became a better friend than I could ever have imagined having. He was much wiser than I was and, as a result, he gave up drugs not long after those early days of sniffing cocaine.

After selling the Kerala cannabis oil, which paid for my last trip to Sri Lanka, I was hooked on the easy money that drug dealing offered. I needed a new business, so I borrowed five grams of cocaine from a Welsh couple who dealt in drugs locally. I started selling it at a small profit. For the first year, I didn't cut it with anything, ensuring that the quality was high and that people would begin to know me for that. But after the first year I started cutting it with about 20 per cent manitol, a harmless baby laxative. Still the quality was still better than local cocaine sold in nearby bars, and this guaranteed that customers would still come back every time. The owner of the Ned Kelly Café didn't mind me doing a bit of business there as long as I was discreet. It became my 'work' for the next eight years. There was no drug squad to worry about in 'relaxed' Holland.

A year later, after one of many returns to India and Sri Lanka had left money tight, a huge bear of a Dutch biker named Marlon offered me 100 g of cocaine on loan. I was broke and needed to start up my business again. His was always top quality, and that was why I was able to start cutting it to make a better profit. The cocaine usu-ally came in crystallised 'rock' form, which I processed in an American hand mill purpose-made for grounding cocaine fine enough to snort. I used tiny greaseproof packets called 'Snow Seals' to put the cocaine in. Five-gram, spring-loaded 'pipe' scales gave me the exact quar-ter-gram divisions that I needed. These dealers' 'kits' were freely available to buy in the 'head shops' of Amsterdam.

My day usually started around noon, when I'd awake from my late night out. I'd watch TV until three, then most days I'd go to the swimming pool for an hour, usu-ally on my bicycle. I swam forty lengths each time, which added up to a kilometre. For ten years, this was my way of keeping fit and counterbalancing all that hard living. Freshened up by my swim, I'd buy an English newspaper and settle down to some beers at Ned's. Usually after three or four beers, I'd take a line of coke. In my pocket would be about five grams in twenty packets of a quarter-gram each. From five in the evening until closing time at 2 a.m. (and often much later), I drank beer and snorted and sold coke, mostly to regulars, while I listened to blues bands that played there until the small hours. Quite how

I managed to survive a lifestyle like that for such a prolonged time, God alone knows.

The Ned Kelly Café was draining to the system, but it was
great fun and became my second home. Blues bands played
each Sunday and sometimes – due to intoxication – I was
brave enough to join in and play some lead guitar. A few
times I even sang Howlin' Wolf's famous blues song 'Evil'.

I could easily emulate his rasping smoky voice because
of all the smoking, 'tooting' (snorting) and drinking that I
did. Yet such an ability meant I could have died at any
time because of the pounding my body was taking. Each
time I woke in the morning I rose into a life without hope
and without love. I found temporary comfort in 'ladies of
the night'. I couldn't settle into a steady relationship,
though I had many one-night stands, and paid visits to
the red light area of The Hague. When business was
good, I visited the Mayfair Club on Eland Straat and took
my pick of the 'top' girls on offer.

Often I drank for forty-eight hours because the cocaine
gave me the staying power I needed. The lifestyle took its
toll and I would have to stay at home and recover for at
least two days, eating takeaways and watching TV. Yet, I
would do it over and over again.

I did some work as 'security' for all kinds of outdoors
and indoor events, but drinking, snorting and dealing
were my main pastimes. I was going nowhere and destroy-
ing my body and mind. Each year I would make a New
Year's resolution to give up, but I never succeeded for long.

More adventures

My brother David was working in Zambia, and paid for
me to visit him for six weeks. The country was wonderful, but my main preoccupation was going to the clubs

and bars to pick up women, and in six weeks I had 'success' with eight of them. This was 1984, before the AIDS epidemic began to devastate Central Africa. Had this trip been made a few years later, I would probably be dead from the disease by now.

The biggest excitement of all on that trip was created by a visit to Victoria Falls, on the border of Zambia and Zimbabwe, on the Zambezi River. David had included this trip in the ticket. I checked into a hotel nearby, after flying down south in a twenty-seater Fokker-Friendship plane. I didn't hang around because I was so eager to see the falls, which were only a couple of hundred yards away from the hotel. As I approached, a noise like thunder increased steadily and when I arrived at the clearing through the trees, my jaw dropped in awe as I witnessed the incredible panorama before me. It was a most awesome sight to behold. A fine, misty smoke rose from the falling water creating multiple rainbows. To get a better view, I crossed the bridge over the Zambezi River into Zimbabwe to see the falls from that side. As I was walking over the bridge a train riddled with bullet holes passed from Zimbabwe into Zambia. I wondered how many times it had been attacked in the fight for independence in Zimbabwe.

I took the path through the head-height grass, constantly watered by the fine mist spray created by the volume of falling water. I passed the statue of Dr Livingstone and imagined what it would have been like to discover this place for the first time. As I looked up at the good doctor there was a rustle in the grass close by. Suddenly I saw a brown, white-spotted deer. I didn't move as I watched it grazing only ten yards away. Then I reminded myself that I was in Africa, and that there could be lions or other big cats about. I looked around nervously and started walking back quickly. It was very hot and I walked at a fast pace. Finally, I reached the bridge that would take me back over the mighty Zambezi River to the safety of my hotel room. I hadn't realised that tourists never went on tours across the bridge without guides.

When I got back to Holland, someone had told the social security that I had been on holiday, but I told them a long story and won my case. Holland had been good to me, yet here I was ripping off their system. My conscience had disappeared.

My next adventure was a trip to Australia in 1986, to visit my Uncle Albert and Auntie Joan. I had never met my mother's brother and his family. He had left our home in Clydach before I was born to join the Australian Army. He had adventure in his blood and had wanted to see the world just like I did. He met and fell in love with Joan there and stayed. They had five children together. We had heard about him as children but nobody knew where he was in Australia. He had not been in contact for all those years, but I had managed to track him down now. It was a very special journey for me, although if Albert had known how I'd got the money to come, he probably wouldn't have welcomed me.

I bought a ticket that would enable me to stop off in Sri Lanka for two months and then go on to Australia for six weeks. Again, I lazed on Unawatuna Beach and got drunk every day. I swam regularly to keep reasonably fit, though I am not sure about the state of my pickled liver by that stage. By the time I arrived in Sydney I was very tanned from two months in my beloved Sri Lanka. I checked into a backpacker's hotel in Sydney and hit the street for the nightlife. On the main street in Kings Cross, I found a fortune-teller who was renowned for correctly predicting the future. Curious, I took everything she had on offer: readings from the crystal ball, the cards and my palm. She predicted that I would have a son in my early forties, and also a long spell in prison after that. Then she told me that I would come into fame and fortune. I thought that this was a highly unlikely story, and brushed it away. I felt a little uncomfortable in there though, probably because I had always been wary of fortune-tellers and modern day prophets.

After a week in the Sydney scene I decided it was time to travel to Melbourne to find Albert. It was great to finally meet my long-lost family, and I felt very privileged to be the first one to see them on their own turf. There had been a family reunion of well over a hundred members two years earlier in Swansea, but it was while I had been in Zambia.

The life I described to them was one big lie and deep down I didn't feel good at all, although the famous Aussie alcohol worked wonders on making my conscience evaporate. Despite all that, I thoroughly enjoyed meeting everyone, and especially all my cousins. Being there, albeit briefly, helped to colour in a section of my family tree which I had previously known very little about. It's curious how important that is.

I travelled from there to Adelaide to visit a friend I had met in Thailand a year earlier. He was a heavy drinker too, and we wasted little time in touring the pubs. In the daytime I checked out Adelaide's Olympic swimming pool, which was the best I had ever been in.

I had been away for three months, and the holiday was still not over. On the way to the Snowy Mountains with Auntie Joan to see my cousins, we stopped off in Glenrowan – the town where the infamous Ned Kelly had made his last stand. I spent about £150 on posters and other souvenirs to take back to Ned's in The Hague. I only saw my cousins and their families for a very short time and then went on to Canberra, Australia's capital city, to meet Bronwen, yet another cousin. With all these new faces to meet, it began to feel as if I was the long-lost one!

A sizeable round of farewells was followed by a flight on to Bangkok, capital of Thailand. With its beautiful women, and designer clothes, I knew I would not be able to stay there for long without running out of money. So I didn't stick around in Bangkok and travelled on to the island of Phuket, down in the south of the country. Then, two weeks later it was time to go home. I had to sell my radio cassette recorder to pay for my exit tax at the airport, but to compensate I took advantage of the free drinks on the plane, ordering gin and tonics all the way home.

I had stashed ten grams of cocaine under the floor-boards in my flat before I left and was looking forward to a good snort when I got there, as it had been a long time. It was almost April and everyone was pale from the long winter, while I had the most ingrained tan that I'd ever had. What a life the life of Brian was, said everyone. Yet inside I didn't feel proud, and I was a very lonely man when sober.

Two weeks after I got back to The Hague I heard on the news that a plane that I had flown on had crashed into the sea just off Phuket. It was on its twice-daily flight from Bangkok to Phuket. I checked the ticket I still had and saw that it bore the same flight number. Now most people would have used information like that to take stock of their lives – but not me. I simply decided that it meant I couldn't put a foot wrong. Once again, sex, drugs, blues bands and swimming were the order of the day. My intake of drink and cocaine increased steadily. It was literally a miracle that I survived. I picked up selling cocaine in the Ned Kelly Café again. All the posters and souvenirs of Ned Kelly's last stand from down under bought me some more selling time, but after eight years, I was finally asked to stop, and soon after, someone else took my place. Considering my regular excursions, I couldn't really complain. A year later some friends of mine – Dave and his wife Sharon bought the place and stopped anyone selling drugs on the premises anyway. So what was I meant to do now?

There was work available with an English contractor named Charley Gray in Rotterdam Harbour, cleaning the inside of tankers and insulating other tanks with glass wool for refrigeration. This was really dirty and very hard work, but I did it for a couple of months. Then I started work again for security teams in pop and culture festivals, but continued to claim social security money, cheating the system. I also sold a small amount of coke from my home. Marlon continued to supply me, even when I had no money. He knew he'd always get it eventually.

Dealing with Freddie

It was Joyce, a 25-year-old beauty from Ghana I often visited down in the red light district, who introduced me to Freddie, a jack-the-lad cockney wheeler-dealer who travelled around Europe doing all kinds of shady deals. Joyce phoned me one night and asked if I would meet a man who could be 'good for business'. I agreed, and we met at a café in town. He was short but stocky and seemed very sure of himself.

'I've been looking forward to meeting you Brian,' he said. 'Joyce speaks very highly of you.' After a little more trivial talk like this, he got down to business.

'Can you find me some good quality heroin for a fair price?' I need a half-kilo by this time next week.'

My first thought was to say no, because I'd never had anything to do with the stuff before. It was bad news. It destroyed too many lives. But the chance to grab some quick, easy money was a strong factor in my answer.

'I'll see what I can do, give me a couple of days.'

Two days later I gave him my address. I had found some Tunisian people who owned a café around the corner from my house. I managed to purchase the half-kilo and charged Freddie 1,000 guilders more than the price I'd paid. It was a nice little earner.

Cockney Freddie kept on coming to my house with other proposals after that. We continued to meet while he was going out with Joyce. She milked him for his money and he didn't know that I was sleeping with her as well. AIDS was around, but it didn't bother me at all. I could almost feel a dark but perversely comforting force urging me on.

One day Freddie surprised me by offering me a trip to India. Would I bring back some heroin, he asked. As I said, I'd always avoided heroin up to this point. I didn't want to get involved in the stuff, but I still needed money desperately. Just at that time, an old acquaintance of mine named Leo came onto the scene. He was a tall, thin Englishman with a softly-spoken cockney accent, and he happened to be in my flat on the day Freddie made his proposal. Leo became interested in going too, and I put this to Freddie, who agreed to send us both.

A week later, we were on our way to New Delhi where we stayed for a couple of days. Then we went on to Agra to visit the Taj Mahal and the Red Fort. After a little sight-seeing, we returned to New Delhi and bought 150 grams of white heroin from some English junkies we had met at a market. Freddie had wanted at least 300 grams to be able to make a good profit, but we realised that we had been spending too much and we would have some explaining to do. The plan to take back what we had managed to buy to Holland was for me to either swallow it or put it inside me. First though, Leo wanted to go to Manali in the North. He smoked a lot of hashish and wanted to go there to buy some and see for himself a place that he had so often heard about.

A week later, after a staggering Himalayan adventure, we left for the airport. Leo wrapped the heroin in some sandwich bags, bound it in sellotape and finally squeezed the lot into condoms. It was ready to put inside me, but when the day came to leave I got scared and couldn't go through with it. I lost my nerve, and Leo wouldn't do it either. After worrying and fretting about what to do, we finally gave the lot to a French junkie in Manali who was flying back a few days after us, and who promised to give it back to us in Europe. It was either that or attempt to sell it there, but we had no time left and the whole thing was too risky. The move we made was a very stupid one of course and, predictably, we never saw him again.

Meanwhile, Freddie, who had set it all up, had to settle for compensation of £1,000, which was only a third of what he'd laid out on the venture. He was very angry with me and I was lucky that he let me off so lightly – he could have easily shot me. He even allowed me to pay him back over a few weeks!

Another opportunity came when Leo's business contact Oliver, who lived in Paris, proposed that he would take a hundred grams of coke from me, and paid me back as he sold it. I agreed, mainly because I was getting increasingly desperate for money, and because it would be no problem starting this business without ready cash – Marlon, my supplier gave me 100 g again on trust.

I brought the coke to Paris, and this time I did put it inside me. The six-hour journey was excruciatingly painful. I checked into a hotel outside the Gare Du Nord (North Train Station). Oliver sold it in a few weeks and all three of us made good money on the deal. My cut was between £1,500–£2,000 about every six weeks, sent on by post. We carried on this business for almost four years leading into the 1990s. I changed my appearance each time so that the train's police detectives would not become familiar with me. As I never got used to the pain, I learned to drink a lot to ease it. It became a nice little earner for a few years, until we tried a bigger deal, and Oliver decided not to pay me. He disappeared with my £4,300 and I never saw him or Leo again. I was wiped out and borrowed some more coke to pay the debt. I bounced back with another plan. I got in touch with some German friends I had met in Sri Lanka. They agreed to shift some coke in their home town in Bavaria, although that particular venture didn't last long.

Social security wised up, and told me they would stop my money if I didn't get a job. So I applied for one as a home help, three days a week. I had six lovely old people to look after: cleaning, shopping and giving them any other help that they needed. I enjoyed this work very much. During this time, an Irish guy who drank in the Ned Kelly Café asked me if I would work on his club's door for two nights a week from nine until four, and I agreed. The unusual contrast between those two jobs as doorman and care worker seemed to balance my life out a little for three years. But I was far from the straight and narrow; I still continued to snort coke and sell a small amount. I consumed large amounts of alcohol to give me the confidence I needed to do my night job. I thought nothing of consuming a six-pack of beers or a bottle of wine two hours before I started at 9 p.m. Then I was onto the gin and tonics while I worked – I needed two days off to recover before I could move on to the home help stuff! I wore a dicky bow, white shirt and black suit and never got hit in three years. With a brain full of coke and alcohol, my gift of the gab increased, and I discovered a propensity for diplomacy. I realised very quickly how important it was not to embarrass anyone in front of their mates or their girl. I knew that if a man's pride was hurt he could come back one day very bitter and stab or even shoot me (there were many guns available on the black market but I kept well clear of them).

Those were crazy days. Looking back, I wonder how on earth I got away with so much. Anyway, my love of easy money was continuing to grip. My involvement in drug-dealing went on and on – the next episode was when I was put in touch with some people in Amsterdam who were organising hashish runs from Kathmandu (in Nepal) to Amsterdam. They needed couriers and, as usual, I was willing. I was to travel to Nepal via a Bangkok stop-over in Thailand for a few days. Then I'd go on to Kathmandu and relax for two weeks while hashish was packed into amplifiers, tuners and other electrical equipment. All I had to do was bring the cases home.

My first trip to Kathmandu was incredibly exciting – again, I was getting a chance to fulfil my desire to see the world while working. As we approached the majestic snow-capped Himalayas, Mount Everest came into view from the plane. I had seen the Himalayas in India from Manali, but they were even more spectacular from the air.

I was given $100 a day to use as I wanted. Normally this would mean a trip to the casino, but at one point I saved two days' money and went to an Indian tailor's shop to be fitted with a very high quality suit for $200. It would have cost $2,000 in the West, and I bought it for my homeward journey, which would be in first class. Being a first class passenger was something I'd always wanted to experience.

I was going through customs when I was unexpectedly stopped and asked to open my case. Customs officers in military uniforms, and armed with AK-47 machine guns approached me. I had to think quickly and stay calm. Luckily I had drunk a quarter-bottle of Johnny Walker before I left the Kathmandu guesthouse, and this stilled my nerves.

'Open the case!' barked one of the soldiers.

I did as he asked. He poked around a little, then looked up at me.

'What is this equipment for?' he growled, pointing at the amplifiers.

'I've been recording wildlife near the foothills of Everest for a documentary,' I answered confidently. Then, before he could go on, I pulled a book out of my pocket - a book entitled *Fearless Ghurkhas* that I had picked up at the hotel and had been reading. I held it up and with a big smile on my face, launched into:

'Ghurkha soldiers are the best in the world. They are the only foreigners who are trusted as personal bodyguards to my Queen in the UK. Nepalese people are very special to us British.'

A couple of the ten or so other soldiers sitting behind these two were listening and got up and applauded me. They told their colleagues to close my case.

'Thank you very much sir for the compliment,' he smiled. 'Some of us are from Ghurkha villages!'

I took a deep breath and smiled broadly. Putting my palms together I offered the Nepalese greeting, Namaste, and went on my way. That was a close one. There were twenty-three kilos of black 'temple ball' Nepalese hashish in my two cases.

The flight home was very interesting, especially the caviar, sour cream, cheese board and 20-year-old ruby port. I had lots of room in my wide seat with fold-out video screen and choice of twelve different movies. I ordered champagne, gin and tonics and expensive whisky, and chatted with a retired Nepalese General who was going on business to Dubai. By the time I got to Holland, fourteen hours later, I was singing and whistling my way through customs. I felt like I was on cloud nine. The adrenaline was pumping again but I was so high from all the alcohol that I was not nervous at all. Maybe that's why no one suspected me. Getting through the Schiphol Airport customs was no problem. Even if I'd been caught, a new law had just been introduced meaning that you could be caught with up to 25 kilos of soft drugs and not be locked up. That's another reason why I felt so carefree.

The pay was 1,000 guilders a kilo. My contacts were waiting to bring me to a 'safe house' to empty the contents of the cases. With the rate of exchange at 2,30 guilders at the time, my kilos earned me £10,000, the most money I had ever held in my hands.

The urge came to travel again, and since I now had the money to go anywhere, I decided to go to Sri Lanka again. It had become my regular place to chill out and have a break from cocaine. I had been there six times already, and on this, my seventh visit, I tried some heroin. I was bored one night and I thought I could take some without getting hooked. I'd never even liked the stuff anyway – I was literally just experimenting out of boredom. There were only a couple of weeks before flying back to Holland, and I was sure I'd be able to stop then . . . . That's what I thought, anyway.

In fact, the first thing I did when I got back was to look for a street dealer to sell me some heroin. I was hooked! From then on, I found myself descending an even steeper, even more slippery slope. I still had money over and now that I was a 'real' junkie, (I didn't think I was one before) I knew I'd need plenty more. And just then, my messed-up brain thought up a scheme to double the money I had earned from my trip to Nepal.

The idea was to take a friend on my eighth visit to Sri Lanka and bring back some heroin. This was another of my hair-brained ideas, yet I went ahead with it . . . and it went wrong and all the money was stolen. My final visit there was destined to go wrong – I had never smuggled drugs from Sri Lanka. It had become a special haven for me, and I should never have tried to spoil that. Somehow, I was glad that I got ripped off. I had always hated heroin, but now, here it was sucking me in like fumes down a tube. And because of its intoxicating enchantment, I'd lost any borderlines that were left; I'd gone into free fall.

The woman I needed?

Becoming increasingly lonely during this time, I remember praying for a proper wife to share my life and have children with. Again, I don't know why I prayed – I just did it randomly for about four months. And it was then that I met Marie Claire at a dealer's house. As I've already explained, she was a beautiful half-Moroccan and half-Dutch girl who was intelligent enough to speak five languages. Looks and brains, and she offers to do my cleaning! Of course I thought it was a good idea! As I said – she was mine within two cleaning trips; we fell for each other almost instantly and she moved in with me.

I was still chasing the dragon on the foil. Heroin was now an ingrained part of my life that I couldn't detach myself from. Though I was only taking about a gram a fortnight, it did not make for a sound platform on which to start a relationship. It got worse though, and my intake soon increased to five grams a fortnight. By the time I was arrested, I was going through five grams every three days.

Soon after Marie Claire moved in, I was offered another trip to Nepal. This time it was not going to be as easy, because getting hold of heroin there (the first time it was just hashish) was a problem. For this reason, I could barely function properly, and it was pretty lucky that I managed to pull off the deal. It was even more of a wonder that the customs officers in Kathmandu or Amsterdam didn't spot my pin-prick pupils, which the heroin had kindly given to me as a side-effect gift. In Kathmandu Airport, I fell asleep in the queue waiting to go through customs. When your body needs heroin, sleepiness is one of the first clues you get.

Marie Claire had lived as a lodger in a dealer's house and was already addicted to crack cocaine. Slowly but surely my participation in and desire for drug-taking increased as well. The money began to slip through our fingers like water now. Desperate for a cash boost, I contacted the men for another trip to Kathmandu. I was lucky because they needed more couriers. Marie Claire begged me to let her come this time, and although at first I refused because it was too dangerous, she nagged me non-stop and finally I relented. After we arrived, I spent most of my time there looking for heroin to feed my craving, as I hadn't been able to afford to buy enough in Holland to take with me. I got sick and the trip organisers found me out. They told me that I wouldn't be asked to do this work again.

Somehow, though, I managed to complete the trip without being found out by the authorities. My first class flight was before Marie Claire's and I had no choice but to leave her there, not knowing at that time that she was a few days pregnant. She reassured me that she was OK – that she would manage – but she became sick just after I left. Then she waited five days longer for her flight. It was a bad and lonely experience for her. I hadn't known the extent of her psychiatric problems, or indeed that she was pregnant. I had thought that we would be travelling back together, not on different flights. When she arrived at Schiphol, Amsterdam, she walked right past me, clearly very upset that I had left her there. I realised that letting her go on the trip had been a very naive decision.

It was a serious falling out, and she even moved back into the crack dealer's house; although she had asked me to keep the money she had earned under my bed. She came around to collect some every few days, and I know she was spending it all on crack. The dealer where she lived told her I had all kinds of diseases. He was trying to get her to stay permanently in his house because he was missing her business. I tried to make her realise this, but it took a while. After she'd bought the cocaine they'd sit there and smoke it with her, meaning that they were basically being paid to take drugs. The child that she was pregnant with – our baby – must have suffered in her womb.

Marie Claire moved back in after they had sucked all the money from her. She'd had four previous abortions and now was contemplating another. I realised that these probably explained why she had needed psychiatric treatment and medication over the years. She would not talk much about her past but I knew that from an early age she'd had some pretty traumatic experiences with men. I realised that pregnancy was making her feel uncomfortable and unhappy again, and I also realised that my addiction was contributing to her angst. I wanted to improve our situation, and also to ensure that she didn't abort our child, so I checked into a detox clinic in The Hague.

Our son, who we decided to name Sonny Ray, had been conceived in the Kathmandu Guesthouse in Nepal and was due to be born at the end of November 1995. Both of us made a great progress staying off drugs for a while and my methadone programme was ongoing. But then, almost inevitably, the downward spiralling began again. Marie Claire started staying away from home to smoke crack, and got into debt with many street dealers. Each time she would disappear for several days, and as I frantically searched for her I would miss the methadone treatments that were helping me to get off the drugs.

Once, after four days searching, I spotted her in the window of a guy's flat barely 500 yards from my own. This guy she was with had knocked on my door a couple of times asking for her. Clearly he was just using her. I rang the bell repeatedly but there was no answer. I got so mad that I kicked a panel out of the door and broke in. I was going to run upstairs when the friend who I was with told me to stay outside while he went up to get her. It was probably a wise suggestion – as it was I just shouted upstairs to the guy to stay away from her. I led her home and she was afraid that I was going to hurt her. She needed help and was crying that she wanted to stop taking drugs but just couldn't, no matter how hard she tried.

After bringing her home, she just wanted to go out again to find more crack. I did my best to keep her there, and even phoned her grandparents hoping they could convince her to listen. They came and talked for a while, but she had heard it all before and when they left it was just a few days before she disappeared again.

One day, in a desperate state of addiction, the deteriorating – but still beautiful – Marie Claire stole the rent and energy money out of my pocket while I was in the shower. I hadn't heard her coming in with her crack-smoking companion, a Nigerian girl who was even more addicted than her. I panicked when I discovered the money was gone and ran out after her. She had already been out for three nights before she stole it. I was so worried that our unborn baby would die or be permanently handicapped. I know she was worried too but, because of the strong pull of addiction she could do very little to stop it. I ran around the corner three streets away and spotted them just in time going into a derelict house. The door was slightly ajar and I ran upstairs and burst into the first room I came to, crying out to her to give me back my money and come home.

There were about six Africans on the first floor.

'Where are the women who just came in?' I shouted, disturbing their peace and making them angry.

But I was far angrier than they were. I told them she was carrying our baby, and that they shouldn't sell her any more crack cocaine.

'I don't have any money Brian,' she lied.

'I'm not stupid Marie Claire – where is it?' I demanded.

'I spent it,' she pleaded feebly.

'But you only just came through the door. I saw you!'

I told her that I heard them coming into my flat when I was in the shower. As soon as I was dressed, I realised that my rent money had gone and chased after them. I tried to put my hand into her pockets but she fought desperately to stop me. After a little persuasion, she gave up the struggle and handed over 100 guilders. That meant there were at least 300 missing!

I was only able to get a quarter of the money back, but I couldn't get her to come home with me. They had spent the rest with the African dealers before I'd arrived and though I tried desperately, I couldn't find the crack they had bought. I became so afraid for Marie Claire and the baby that I called to a shopkeeper to phone an ambulance while I tried to hold on to her. There was a struggle in the street and I accidentally bumped her abdomen. She was bent over in pain as the ambulance arrived. Panicking, I tried to get her to go to the hospital, but she wouldn't. I insisted that if they didn't take her, our baby could die (I was of course terrified by now that the bump I had given her in the struggle, coupled with the bombardment of drugs into Marie Claire's system may have already killed the baby). They stressed that they couldn't do anything without her consent. She shouted that it was finished between us and told me to leave her alone. Realising I could do nothing, I waved the medics on their way, and trudged off home.

Marie Claire eventually came home about six hours later saying she was very sorry. She was exhausted and went to sleep. I called her mother and grandparents to come and help, but they were tired of the same old story after trying to help her for so long. This time they all threatened to disown her if she didn't stop the drugs. At that point, due to the compound shock of that threat and the hideous fights and arguments of those past few weeks, we both stopped taking drugs again. This time we managed to last for a few months until just after the baby was born on 10th October 1995.

We were required to attend interviews with social workers before and after Sonny Ray's birth, six-weeks premature. He was put on a drip for a week and stayed in hospital for another five weeks before the social services decided we were doing well enough to have him home. This was just two weeks before I was arrested in Swansea. In the six weeks that he was in hospital, Marie Claire and I had slowly but surely become ensnared by the drugs again, and three weeks after our son was born, I missed my methadone prescription yet again because I was out searching for her.

Cold turkey came upon me in a rush, and I was unprepared for it. I managed to persuade the Turkish dealers give me 5 g on loan again very cheaply. Then I 'chased the dragon' on the aluminium foil, sucking eagerly at the hot, smoking, bubbling brown liquid vapour through a makeshift tube and feeling the numbing effect take hold again. My lighter would run out of gas and I would curse because I had no money left to buy a new one, so then the gas stove became my source of flame. Sometimes my moustache would catch light, but I couldn't feel any pain because of the powerful narcotic. I scratched myself constantly; my body always itched all over. This time, I had completely lost control. We'd both been so desperate to get out of it, but instead, once again, we only found ourselves deeper and deeper in this great pit we'd dug for ourselves.

Sonny Ray was released into our care because we had somehow managed to look healthy enough at the meetings with the social worker. If they had known much about our condition, our son would not have been allowed to come home. We were so happy to have him, and again became determined to get our lives sorted. This time we even decided to move out of the area and get married; make a fresh start.

Of course I couldn't quite make that fresh start, not just yet. I owed 4,000 guilders to the Turkish dealers in The Hague, and they were putting the pressure on. Ahmed was trying to convince me that a trip – to Britain – was the best way forward; Joe was phoning from Wales to say that he 'could shift anything I could bring'; and I had a brand new family that desperately needed a strong man who could lead them out of misery.

But that's not how it turned out. Instead, I ended up sitting in a police station cell – cold, shaking and miserable, but slowly realising what I was, and how lucky I was even to be alive. The last twenty years had been a gigantic cocktail of drugs, crime and fast living – and much of my recent past had been horrible. But any feelings of regret I may have had simply paled into insignificance, once compared to the terrifying prospects that lay in the future.

SIX

Rock bottom

I was not allowed to see anyone while I was being questioned in the police station, though I was able to make one phone call to Marie Claire in Holland, and she was also allowed to call me twice. It caused me great anxiety to think that she was alone with Sonny Ray over in Holland because, in the few weeks leading up to my arrest, many different hustlers had been coming to the door asking for her. I had turned most of them away telling them to leave us alone now that we were trying to get our lives together. Marie Claire had met these people during her search for crack houses and had probably smoked a lot of it with them. Now they were at her door, and knew of my arrest. I knew they would be helping themselves to my belongings to sell for crack. What also concerned me was that Marie Claire was in possession of my bank pass. Before I'd left we'd just received our first joint payment as a couple from the social services of about 1,800 guilders (£750 then), to cover a month. I knew that this would be used up in no time, along with all my items of value. On the phone, she told me that they were taking everything, and that she was afraid. I could do nothing to help her; I couldn't even contact my brother Raymond, who was living about a mile away, because I had forgotten his number! I didn't care about my things any more, but I was full of guilt and concern for my family's safety. I was in a mess because of it! It was a nightmare realising that the situation was getting worse, and I could do nothing about it – I wasn't even allowed to write letters. What would become of Marie Claire and Sonny Ray, I fearfully wondered?

It was time for me to be questioned. For the next four hours, I was shut in a tiny room, sitting with two officers and a 'duty solicitor'. I was weak and always on the very verges of sleep. Everything was strange in this dark, sober world. Voices echoed at me from no particular direction, and in spite of the damaged state my mind was in, I did my best to tell the truth. Well, mostly. I was keeping Joe Roberts out of it – telling them that I had been the one who was trying to sell the drugs for Ahmed. Apart from that, the rest was true. After all, it was me who had smuggled cocaine into the country from Holland. Joe didn't need to get dragged down with me. I told them about the whole journey except the part about turning up at Joe's so that he could sell the drugs. Instead, I made up a story that I had tried to sell the cocaine in Clydach pubs – even though that was a more serious offence that would result in a much heavier sentence. I told them that a taxi had brought us to Clydach and stopped outside a local pub, which was absolutely true. I didn't tell them, of course, that Joe lived two doors away.

I was taken back to my cell and a second doctor came to see me because I kept pleading with the police. He sat with me and talked for a while, seeming concerned with my condition. He asked me how much methadone I'd received when detoxing in Holland.

'75 ml,' I told him.

'That's a lot!' he yelped, taken aback.

He wouldn't prescribe anywhere near that much, and no matter how much I protested, he only gave me 10 ml. It gave me a little relief but by no means enough. It was like suffering a heart attack and being given a couple of paracetamol.

After a microwave meal of curry and rice, which I threw up, it was back for questioning. Marie Claire phoned after that at about 10 p.m. She sounded so worried. When I got back to the cell, it hit me hard. I had caused many people a lot of pain. The cold, stark reality of my plight in that dark, lonely police cell, was heavy upon me. I was filled with despair, self-pity, guilt and shame…

My life began to play out before me, and for the first time I seriously considered taking my own life. Then I felt the reality of what I had done and the people I had hurt, very heavily. I cried for Sonny Ray and Marie Claire, and for my brothers and sisters who would have heard of my arrest by now. I was front-page news, and my face was all over the television. I knew that my stepfather Ray's house had been raided at the same time as we were arrested, and that he was in a state of shock from the fright. He had never been in trouble with the police before. His house in Clydach had been turned upside down. They had picked on him because I had given his address to the hotel reception. That's where I usually stayed when I came home to visit. Now I had really blown it with my family.

I shook and cried uncontrollably and thought again of suicide. Out of the corner of my eye I spotted a plastic knife, and in desperation I even attempted cutting my wrists with it as I sobbed. Of course it wasn't hard or sharp enough; it only made sore scratch marks.

Released while detained

Even as I was attempting to take my life, I realised that this was an easy, selfish way out. I sat there wondering if there was a God watching down over me as I contemplated the end. Deep down, I think I knew that he was.

I remembered the time when Steve, who had shared our squat in London, had dragged me along to this little church in Swansea where many people were miraculously getting healed from all kinds of addictions. It was a run down little place that had seen better days, but as we walked in it was filled with beautiful singing. Steve ushered me down near the front. It was packed out with people with their hands raised. 'I love it here Brian,' beamed Steve, 'this is my family.'

The singing stopped and the preacher started praying. He asked what he called 'the Holy Spirit' to move among the audience. I wasn't sure what this meant, but as I wondered, Steve spontaneously started saying the strangest things – as if he'd flipped his lid. I opened my eyes and stared at him, listening in amazement. He was saying something like 'Alamunda kaiunda bashinda' – I've always remembered how those words sounded ever since that day. He explained afterwards that he was 'speaking in tongues' – talking fluently in a foreign language bestowed suddenly upon him from above. We had been best mates for years, so I knew he wasn't faking it.

I had often experienced answers to prayers in my life. I had believed in God – the God of the Bible actually – since I was a small child. I'd tried to become a Christian in Kerry Jenkins' house when I was eighteen, just after our run-in with the police at The Kingdom in Clydach.

We'd had a bad trip that night and we thought we'd had some kind of religious experience. We believed that we could 'float' in the 'astral plain' and the amount of LSD that we took that night really spaced us out. I believe now that we were unwittingly tapping into a spirit world that we knew nothing about. There was a point when we seemed to come upon a door, and then going beyond that door there was only blackness.

The police had told us to go home, but many of us decided to go and visit Kerry, a local lay preacher. Kerry let over twenty of us into his house without fear for his family's safety. He was happy to help and share his view of what had happened to us that night. His wife Morwen put the kettle on and made tea and biscuits for us all.

I was not as afraid as many of the guys were and listened as they explained about the strange LSD trip that they had experienced that night.

'We were floating in a sea of tranquillity, it was like we were one with the earth Kerry, until we came to the black abyss on the other side of the door,' explained Steve (the one who spoke in tongues a couple of years later).

Kerry told us that there were only two spiritual dimensions, that of good and that of evil – that of light and that of darkness – and that evil and darkness can deceive and confuse. He said that good was from God who was in the light, and not to be found in the darkness and confusion that we had spoken of. He asked if he could pray for us and we all readily agreed. After that, Kerry asked us if we wanted to 'give our hearts to Jesus'. And together many of us stammered the 'sinner's prayer', which entailed being sorry for all the things that we had done wrong in our lives and then asking Jesus into our hearts to come and live there so that we could be saved from the power of sin. I think I was pretty sincere at that moment.

Some of the other guys who were there that night became committed Christians, turning their backs on drugs and drink. Two of them, including Steve, even went on to become church pastors. But as for me – well, as you know by now, that was a different story. My ravenous desire for the pleasures of the world were not satisfied and I couldn't live a lie. I soon drifted back to my old ways, even though I didn't doubt that what Kerry had told us that night was true. I just made a choice.

Now, twenty-five years later, I had my reward. Here I was, going through the hell of cold turkey in a police station cell. I was full of shame and fear, and I genuinely felt like ending it all. I was in the most desperate and pathetic state I've ever been in. I'd hit rock bottom.

So I did the only thing I could. I prayed. I cried out to God for help. I realised that I was only still alive because God had not allowed me to die, and so I called out to him in a small, meek voice, and asked him to intervene. Nothing spectacular happened, but my cold turkey eased and I was able to think more clearly and feel a little better. I felt a sense of hope rising. I was still sick, but not as badly as before.

I knew then, in my heart, and not just in my head, that I had to change. I had tried so many times before but never succeeded, but now it felt that I had no other way left to go. It was as if God had caused me to be arrested because it was the only way to save me from an inevitable death. I felt as if I was being shaken awake. Why not give God a chance, I thought to myself?

I asked him to show me clearly that he was there, with me in that cell. I waited for some sort of spiritual experience from God – like Steve's weird tongue thing – but there was nothing at first. Yet when I thought about it, I realised that the fear, which had practically paralysed me since I'd been in custody, had left me. I was not afraid anymore – and that was some sort of miracle! Then I realised that if I was going to be following God from now on, I would have to tell the police the absolute truth, with no lies. It's hard to explain why, but this is what I felt he wanted me to do.

Locked up

We had been arrested on a Friday and locked up over the weekend until appearing in Swansea Magistrates Court on the Monday morning. I had entered a guilty plea and Ahmed had pleaded not guilty. We were remanded in custody to appear again just over a week later. Ahmed looked solemn as we were taken to the cells below the court.

'Brian, you say to police I come for Christmas holiday, no?' he whispered. 'I give you £25,000, you say I not know nothing. After, Marie Claire and Sonny Ray have money, no problem yes?'

He was playing on my weakness and it was hard for me to explain to him that I had to tell the truth. So I told him that he couldn't get away with it because the coke was found in a hotel room where we both were, and that if we lied and went to trial, we could get a much longer sentence. It would be better if he just told the truth and pleaded guilty straight away like I had done. Ahmed decided that he was going to fight it. How he was going to do that was a mystery to me.

I had been hoping to see my brother Chris. He was eight years younger than me, and had lived in Clydach all his life. He had spent many years in prison for shop-lifting and for attacking a policeman who made him angry. The policeman had always intended to get Chris to lose his rag and it had worked. That local policeman had a grudge against him and swore he would get him one day. He came to ask a few questions at the door of Chris's flat, and when Chris asked him to leave, he put his foot in the door and barked out some very insulting words about Mam, who'd recently passed away. That was it! Chris grabbed an axe and chased after the cop, who ran for his life and dived into his panda car just before the axe penetrated the roof, missing his head by inches. He got his longest prison stretch for that. It was four years. That was the final straw for Chris and he stayed out of trouble after that.

Chris came to my cell under the courts while I was awaiting trial. He was with my sister Wendy and, without anyone suspecting, slipped me a third of a bottle of vodka mixed with orange. He had avoided trouble for so long, and now he was prepared to risk his freedom so that I could have some relief. He would have even taken my place in prison if that were possible. I looked at the bottle and realised that for the first time in ten years I had not had a drink for more than three days. I quickly drank it down, before I could be caught. It went down so well and gave me a warm feeling, far better than 10 ml of methadone could. It helped me cope with leaving for Swansea prison an hour later.

I had often passed the prison and even visited Chris there once, ten years earlier. Now it was going to be my home. I looked out of the tinted window at the side of the prisoner van from my 'sweatbox' (compartment within the van) as we drove through the old prison gateway arch. The huge doors crashed shut behind us, and we were led out of the van to the reception door. The tiny waiting room was really dirty, with half-empty plates of the most disgusting looking food lying around, and with new inmates waiting their turn to be registered. Finally, after about an hour's wait, the guard shouted 'Morris!' and it was my turn to be dealt with.

'Empty your pockets on the table, Morris.'

I only had some tobacco and a lighter.

'You will be RX 1112 from now on.'

The man before me must have been RX1111. That was some special number to miss, I thought!

'Right, take your clothes off, get into that shower and then put these on,' he ordered.

A 'privileged' inmate handed me some old jeans and T-shirt. I did as I was told, then joined the rest of the new lads, waiting in another room for half an hour. Then the guard returned:

'Lets get you lot kitted up and onto the wing. This way boys.'

We were handed a roll of blankets, plastic eating and drinking utensils and toiletries. Our T-shirts, jeans, underwear and socks were rolled up in the blankets. Ahmed and I were led to the second floor of A-Wing and placed in a cell together. I hadn't wanted this, because he kept on moaning at me that I was coughing a lot and had a big problem with sleeping. We had never been mates and now, because everything had gone wrong and I was reluctant to lie for him, he mixed with other inmates and kept his distance from me. We only shared the cell for a week: that was until our next court appearance. This was to extend our bail for a further three weeks. They read out the charges again, but this time there was some new information about Ahmed. I heard that he was wanted in Holland for shooting a man in the knees.

It was 18th December 1995 when we arrived at Swansea prison. My 42nd Birthday was just three days later. I was very lonely and missing my young family so much. I was down and depressed – these were the most miserable days I had ever experienced. Christmas came and went very quickly. I had put the Christmas tree and decorations up a week before I left Holland. It would not be much of a Christmas for Marie Claire and Sonny Ray. I wrote letters but received no replies. My sisters rang my number in Holland many times but no one picked it up. I had no prison phone cards to call her myself – because I had no money. When I did finally earn the money to buy a card, and called, I found that my phone had been cut off. It meant that I had no contact with Marie Claire at all, and it made my time very hard.

Our next visit to the Magistrates Court in January was called off at the last minute because of a bomb scare. The police had received an anonymous phone call and it was taken very seriously. It was believed that Ahmed's Turkish friends were behind it, so he was immediately moved to an 'A' category prison in Bristol. This helped me to stick by my decision not to lie for him to try and get him off. If I had made up a story, lying for him to say that he had had nothing to do with the drugs, I was sure I would receive a much longer sentence.

Before he was moved, Ahmed had spread the word that I was unwilling to cover for him. The other inmates now believed that I was a grass, and so life became even harder for me. I had to watch my back in case I was stabbed, or someone threw boiling sugared water in my face (sugar was used to increase the intensity of the burn, and boiling water with a lot of sugar mixed in could do a lot of permanent damage). Prison justice could come swiftly at any time. Word spreads fast and most inmates believe every rumour to be the absolute truth.

All this time I had been reading my Bible and praying. As I read, I found myself continually delivered from fear, comforted by the thought that God could talk to me through these words. I read a verse, Hebrews 13:6, that said: 'The Lord is my helper; I will not be afraid. What can man do to me?' It couldn't have been more real if God had spoken out loud to me. My whole attitude changed, and I just trusted that he would protect me. How could anyone hurt me when God was on my side? That is what I believed in my heart. I now felt that I had nothing to worry about.

When I read my Bible I learned a lot about Jesus Christ. I hadn't really realised this before, but Jesus was certainly the greatest revolutionary who ever lived. When he was walking around, two thousand years ago, he was upsetting all sorts of people with his words and actions, so much so that they gave him the death penalty to silence him. The Bible told me that he died on the cross in order to change the course of history, and then came back to life three days later, which he was able to do because he was actually the Son of God. It was mind-blowing stuff.

I was given a job as a cleaner and set out to do the best I could do, trying hard to be a good Christian and to do even the most menial of tasks with pride. I was still feeling very hurt and angry – there were many issues to be dealt with in my life. It was only the beginning of my Christian journey. I had not told anyone yet about my decision in Swansea Police Station. That was hard, because it was the one good thing that had happened to me recently – but I was afraid of being ridiculed. So I just quietly slipped off to chapel every Sunday. It was called the 'Upper Room' because it was on the first floor of another building in the prison. It wasn't very big, and between ten and twenty inmates attended each week, meaning it was rarely more than half full.

New inmates were offered a job soon after arrival and it was advisable not to refuse any work because otherwise you'd be locked up all the time, and you'd even miss out on 'association' five nights and two weekend afternoons each week. This meant that for two hours at a time, we could watch TV, play snooker, pool and table tennis or use the library. Having taken the cleaning job, I was allowed out in the morning and afternoons to clean for a few hours and for association. Once a day we could go into the yard outside for exercise. Inmates just sat about or walked round and round an area half the size of a foot-ball pitch, but when it rained, the whole prison was locked down.

Those of us who went to the chapel on Sundays enjoyed singing together and listening to the sermons given by the prison chaplain, the Revd Ted Hunt, who looked like Batman in his black robes. It was the only really 'happy' place in the prison. Some really loving Christian people attended the service from an organisa-tion called the Prison Fellowship. They told me that they would visit me if I wanted and that they would pray for me as well. They were amazing people, and I had to find out more about them. I found a book in the library about how their organisation came about. I discovered that Chuck Colson, who was Richard Nixon's 'hatchet man' in the Watergate scandal, founded this group, the Prison Fellowship. His spell in prison changed him dramatically after he read C. S. Lewis' book *Mere Christianity*, and he decided to set up a project to bring the Christian message to prison inmates in the US. Obviously things had grown a bit since then, and now Prison Fellowship groups oper-ate all over the world, including Swansea.

An unlikely reunion

A few days after Ahmed was sent to Bristol I noticed that one of the single cells had been vacated. I asked if I could have it and was chuffed when the officer told me I could. I got myself a New Testament from the chaplain. Two weeks later I was amazed one day when I turned into the chaplain's office on A-Wing. I got a huge shock because I saw my old boss on the tarmac gang, Kerry Jenkins, talking to someone just outside the office on our B-Wing. It was the same man who had helped us young hippies on the night of our bad trip – the same man who had so nearly persuaded me to follow Christ when I was just a teenager. I had prayed for a sign from God, confirming that he was with me now, and I knew this was it.

I hadn't seen Kerry since we were both in Clydach all those years ago. I remembered that back then he'd been a real man of God, and it was clear that nothing had changed. He usually talked about nothing other than Jesus, was probably the most honest person I have ever known and yet still felt guilty about his integrity. It seemed that his greatest desire was that he would learn to become more humble, and his prayer for so many years was simply that he could become more and more like Jesus. What a man! I didn't know anyone like him – not only in Clydach, but in the whole of Wales. He was so excited and pleased to see me that he asked if I would come into the office to talk. Revd Hunt got up from his desk and left us alone for a while. Kerry prayed for me and then spontaneously burst into tongues – just like Steve had in that chapel years ago. When he finished, he then interpreted those strange words as if God was speaking directly through him. I was not to be afraid. God was with me and would rebuild my life. I was to trust and obey him and all would go well with me. He had brought me to a point in my life where there was no turning back. Then Kerry asked me to pray, but I couldn't say anything. I was too self-conscious to pray out loud – I had never done it before. All I could do was weep for all the trouble I had caused Marie Claire, Sonny and my family. I was doused in self-pity and shame.

Kerry gave me a copy of a Christian magazine called *Challenge* to take back to my cell to read. In it, I found the address of a Christian counsellor to whom I could write with my problems. I did this and was thrilled when I received a reply. It turned out that this man, Claud Trigger, was 82 years old and had been a preacher for nearly sixty of them, but had lost the use of his voice due to throat cancer. His typed letters were so helpful to me, answering many questions about God, other religions, life and suffering. Even when my letters were a little rude or angry, he still wrote back graciously. This helped me so much in those very difficult first months – along with letters and prayers from Kerry's church. Claud told me that I was always in his prayers. By now, quite a few people were praying for me. I wasn't going to knock this. I needed all the help I could get and deep down I realised that prayer could be very helpful indeed.

David Hamilton, an ex-loyalist terrorist, came to speak in the chapel and told us the amazing story of how he had survived bullets and bombs to become a Christian. I was very inspired, and when he revealed that he had written a book I asked him for a copy. He apologised that it wasn't out in English but that he had a Dutch version. Being able to read Dutch, I proudly announced that this wouldn't be a problem! I read his story, and saw how God can change people who harbour so much anger. I too was very angry and needed to change in that area. Occasionally, when I was upset, I'd punch the cell wall with tremendous force.

I was thinking about how I could tell my family about my faith. I was really embarrassed by it. Even when someone entered my cell I would quickly hide my New Testament, ashamed that they might see it and laugh at me. That was until I saw the verses in the Bible that clearly stated that if I was ashamed of God, then he would be ashamed of me (Mark 8:38 and Romans 1:16). After that, I started to leave my Bible out for all to see.

Kerry came onto the wing again. I never knew when he would be allowed to see us, but I know for sure that he did his best to see as many people as possible. The second time we were together I managed to say a prayer out loud and felt much better for it afterwards. I seemed much more relaxed. Back in my cell, I pulled down the pornographic pictures left by the last occupant and cleaned the cell from top to bottom. Then, excited by this whole new world of faith that I was uncovering, I got stuck into some more Christian testimony books that I'd picked up from the chapel. I would get so inspired during reading that I often shouted out excitedly to God. I got down on my knees each night and prayed until my legs ached and my knees hurt. I also got to know the Prison Fellowship members from around West Glamorgan, who came to chapel every Sunday and often to visit. They told me that they would pray for me. Now I was being supported by a lot of praying people.

One day, while I was cleaning, there was trouble. A man called me a snitch in front of a few lads standing near, and I didn't have the sense to let it go. My pride had been hurt, and I walked up to him and hit him. Then we started fighting, until a couple of officers broke us up. We were both taken to the governor's office, and I was isolated from the wing. I was not allowed any exercise that day. I truly felt sorry for what I had done because I was trying to be a Christian. I apologised to the inmate, Dave Ross, while we were in front of the governor by giving him my hand, which he accepted. I believe that this gesture, and my prayers beforehand, caused the governor to be lenient on us.

'Because it's Easter, I'm only giving you a warning this time, but if you mess up again I'll send you both to a top security prison,' the governor snapped. 'And don't forget, this incident will be put on your records. Now get back to your cells.'

On the way back to our wing Dave Ross growled at me:

'Keep away from me. Don't think that shaking hands meant anything to me. I will not forget this.'

Soon after I noticed that all his mates were ignoring me.

In my defence

I asked for Elwen Evans to represent me as my barrister because I had heard how good she was with mitigation. I had a strong case because of my addiction and the pressure that had been put on me because of my debts. After meeting her a couple of times, she filled me with a lot of hope that I could receive a light sentence.

Having talked with Elwen, I decided to tell the police about arriving in the taxi outside Joe's house and staying there for the day. It had dawned on me that the taxi driver may have told the police that I had met a man when he dropped me off. I still lied about Joe's involvement in the crime. I told them in a new statement that I had stayed in

Joe's house but that he was completely innocent of taking any part in the crime.

I had not heard from Joe since my arrest, but received news from my family that he was in hiding because many people were calling him a grass. The same was happening to Ricky. When I discovered this, I put out the message through my family that they should be left alone. In my heart I knew that I had to forgive them, even if it were true that they had been working for the police. I had no proof of this anyway, and I certainly didn't want to believe it. I started to write to Joe but I didn't write anything about his involvement in the deal because I knew that the officers read my mail. After asking him many times to come to visit, he eventually did, but it was only after my sister Wendy had gone into a pub in Clydach to get him. She told him that if he were innocent, he would not be afraid to speak to me. He had to give in because a lot of local people had overheard their conversation.

When Joe walked into the visiting room he was shaking very badly and looked frightened. I asked him why he was shaking. He told me that he was ill and that his mother was also very sick. He grumbled that everyone was blaming him for setting me up with the police. I gave him the assurance that I had told everyone to leave him alone. He asked why I had changed my statement and told the police about coming to his house? I reassured him that he shouldn't worry, because I didn't tell them anything that would put him in danger of arrest. Then he told me something, which really surprised me:

'Ricky phoned the customs in Harwich,' he said.

I didn't show my shock then, but quietly answered.

'Lucky I gave you false information on the phone then!' I said, grinning.

He shifted nervously. I still didn't want to believe that Joe was guilty of working with the police. But how had Ricky known which way I was coming unless Joe had told him? Joe had told me that Ricky would not be involved and know nothing about the deal between us, but it just didn't add up.

Joe promised that he would get some heavy dealer characters caught for me, in order to get me a lighter sentence. He wrote and told me that he was in regular contact with Inspector Nigel Doxey, who had been the arresting officer in my case. Joe said that he had been in contact with him since I had made my new statement to the police about our arrival from Holland to Joe's house. Now, of course, I was wondering if he had been in contact with Doxey for much longer, even well before my arrest.

He explained that he was in communication with Doxey every week and was getting closer to catching someone for me. Catching someone for me? I just played along, knowing that it was strange for Joe to be in so much contact with the police. It was curious that he was prepared to grass anybody up to help me. I thought that if it was so easy for him to do that against a stranger, then why not against me? There was good money in it for him – I hear the police pay well these days for informants. He had also forgotten that he told me that he had left London in a hurry because of problems with the Metropolitan Police. He had lived in London for many years and suddenly got out because of some drug problem. So maybe the police had something on him? Was it possible he was doing a deal with them to get off? I continued to write to him, but carefully saved each letter that he wrote back.

I had not heard from Marie Claire since my first week in prison and I worried a lot about it. Then I received a letter. It was short and to the point; what they call a 'Dear John' letter. This is what it said:

24th February 1996

Dear Brian,

I'm sorry to inform you that it's over between us. It's not possible for us to go on like this. Sonny is going to foster parents for two years and I am getting my life together. I'm following a detox programme and everything is going fine.

I'm sorry you had to go to prison but I wish you luck. Please take care of yourself. I'm sorry things worked out the way they did.

Greetings,

Marie Claire

That was it – it was finished between us. This hit me hard; I was completely devastated. It was going to prove very difficult for me to let go of Marie Claire. Although the letter was dated 24th February, it had not arrived in my hands until the middle of April. The letter had been sent to my solicitors and they'd mislaid it for a couple of months.

After six months in prison, I received a letter from the Child Care Agency in The Hague, Holland. In it were some photos of Sonny Ray. I had not seen him grow and this both cut my heart and touched me deeply. Tears of joy streamed down my face as I saw how my lovely boy was developing. He was in the arms of his mother who had been on one of her fortnightly visits to the childcare centre. She looked well, if somewhat tired.

But, only a few weeks later, I got a letter from her grandmother saying that Marie Claire had twice tried to kill herself, once with a bottle of tablets not long after my arrest, and again in June just after she turned 29. She cut herself with a broken glass and was admitted to a psychiatric hospital where she stayed for three months. It reminded me so much of Noor and what I had been through with her. This was hard to take in and soon became a worry that ate away at me. Her grandmother wrote that she had often complained, 'I wish Brian was here.' I really believed she still cared for me and I hung on to these words like a link to getting her back. I longed to speak with her but was not allowed to because of her condition.

These were painful days indeed. At least I now had contact with the Child Care Agency who kept me up to date with my son's progress with his new foster family. They had two other foster children aged three and four, which was great news because I'd wanted Sonny to have a brother and sister. The parents were white Catholic Dutch, and the boy and girl – named Vinay and Sushama – were of Asian background. As time went by and more photos were sent, I realised that God had given Sonny a wonderful home that I could not have provided. They clearly loved him very much; he looked so happy in the photos. They brought him once every two weeks to the agency so he could see Marie Claire. To me, Vinay and Sushama looked like Sri Lankan children. This really pleased me, knowing that Sonny wouldn't grow up with any problems with racism. In fact, I wondered if God might be preparing him for visits to Sri Lanka with me, later in life.

SEVEN

Trying times

Seven months after my arrest I was sent to Bullingdon prison in Oxford. This was a newly-built prison, the wings of which were small and brightly coloured. Ours was bright yellow, which was a change from the old Victorian greys and greens of Swansea. There was an Arts & Crafts class operating there that I was able to take advantage of. I had the opportunity to make some cuddly toys and hand puppets, and to send them well in time for Sonny Ray's first birthday, which was on 10th October 1996. My pay was only £5 a week so this was a literal Godsend for me.

Around this time, I received a letter from Joe, asking me about Marlon, my Dutch supplier. He wanted to know whether he was coming to visit me. This made me even more suspicious that Joe was working with the police. I wrote back and answered that I didn't know any-one called Marlon. I had the feeling that he was fishing for information for Inspector Doxey. I had not mentioned Marlon to him, but I remembered that Ricky had met Marlon once on a visit to me in Holland. It was Marlon who had supplied me with cocaine for most of my deal-ing, and I felt that he was a good friend of mine. Ricky was in my flat on a visit to Holland once when Marlon came in with my supply of coke, so I figured that he must have told Joe about him. Were the police trying to find out where the drugs had originated in Holland? Who knows? I played it dead straight in my letters. Joe also told me again about his regular meetings with Inspector Doxey, and said that he was coming close to making an arrest 'for me'. I didn't believe him, but I continued to play along.

From Bullingdon I wrote to my stepfather Ray and apologised as best I could for the police raid on his house. Though I did this a number of times, I received no reply. He was not a letter writer and I hardly expected him to answer, but I knew that he and some of my family were finding it very hard to forgive me. It was a very serious thing I had done to them, and I deserved all of this. I had brought shame and humiliation on them all. I knew that time would act as a healer though and believed that God would eventually restore our broken relationships.

During these emotional and trying days, when I was missing Marie Claire so much, I started writing a lot of poems again, just like the time after Noor left me. It seems that heartache turns me into a poet! Drugs were all around and though I thought I needed some badly, somehow I had the strength to stay away. I prayed that I would be able to stay drug-free, and asked God that the yearning within me for another fix would disappear. Even though I still had the desire for them, I was able to keep away for the first time ever. The combination of prayers and my aspiration to get out of prison as soon as possible gave me the edge I needed. Urine testing was a routine undertaking about once a month; sometimes even two or three times to catch out those who thought they'd beaten the system. I didn't want a positive test to spoil my chances of a lighter sentence and freedom.

I attended chapel regularly each week and enjoyed listening to the people who came in to tell their stories. I read three Christian life-stories from the chapel library each week, and became increasingly convinced that God could completely change and revolutionise lives. As long as I prayed, met with other Christians in church, and cleaned up my life, I believed that I would somehow get a lighter sentence. Then I could rejoin Marie Claire in Holland, and get Sonny Ray out of care.

I applied for a transfer to Swansea or Cardiff so I could prepare my case with my barrister, Elwen. But the answer both prisons gave was: 'unable to accommodate'. I was very annoyed by this because it meant that I would only have a few minutes to see my barrister just before going into the Crown Court. In the end, I was transferred to Swansea on a Friday to appear the following Monday. But even so, I could not see my barrister until I reached court. It seemed that this was the same story that many prisoners faced. Inmates would be transferred away from the location where they were due to be tried a couple of months before their court case, thus losing any advantage of proper preparation.

It was good though to be back in Swansea. I could now see my family again. I had received no visits in Oxford because it was too far away. I had already got to know the officers in Swansea, and one of them had given me a single cell when I asked for it because I had shown respect to him. Most inmates hated those in authority but I knew that was stupid. My Bible told me to love them. So I treated them the same as inmates and never agreed with the 'them and us' ethos. People are people and officers have feelings and families too. I did not 'brown-nose' or 'snuggle up' as some would call it, but I did do my best to please everyone.

Going the opposite way from most of the inmates was not easy – it took a lot of courage. As I soon realised, a

Christian is certainly not a wimp. Showing kindness to officers meant I was walking a dangerous line in the prison environment. Rumours are quick to spread if someone suggests that you are a friend of the guards. Many people were praying for me and perhaps that's why I wasn't harmed during this period. I continued to treat guards and inmates alike, and I really did 'stand' on God's promise in Hebrews 13:6: 'The Lord is my helper; I will not be afraid. What can man do to me?'

Monday morning arrived. We would soon be sitting in the tiny 'sweatbox' of the security van, on our way to court. Ahmed had not been transferred on Friday like me. He arrived direct at the court from Bristol on Monday morning, escorted by six officers. It seemed they were taking him very seriously. Two officers produced me. Elwen Evans came to see me in a holding cell under the court and told me, very apologetically, that she was still in the midst of a murder case which had lasted longer than expected. She told me not to worry, as she had given my case to a very good barrister by the name of James Jenkins. He came to see me in the holding cell just before I was about to appear in court and told me that he had been up all night studying my case. I was really upset that Elwen Evans could not represent me. In my mistrusting mind, it seemed to me that the authorities had set it all up. Mr Jenkins stressed that I had very good mitigating circumstances and thought that I was looking at about five years.

He explained that because there was a dispute about who did what and who was telling the truth, there was to be a 'Newton' trial (a 'Newton' trial is a trial of issue where the judge and not a jury will decide who is telling the truth after hearing different versions of a case) to determine whether my story or Ahmed's was true. He assured me that because I had pleaded guilty at the first opportunity, I would win this dispute easily. Ahmed had first pleaded not guilty and then changed it to guilty.

Trial and error

So at last, here I was in court. I took the stand and though I swore on the Bible to tell the whole truth, I didn't. (Some Christian I was!) I kept Joe and his flatmate's involvement in the crime out of the story and stated that I was the distributor of the drugs. I was very nervous in the dock and my voice and body trembled at such exposure. I had long prayed for this day to come but now I felt so helpless and vulnerable. It didn't feel right lying about Joe, but I didn't want to be known in Clydach as an informer, a grass. I still didn't believe that Joe could be working for the police, even though it seemed so obvious. He would be immune from prosecution anyway, even if the whole truth came out. I thought the police would disclose this information during the trial but they seemed to be happy with the evidence as it was, and it appeared that my story was better for them. That way, they didn't have to disclose to the court that they had used someone to entice me into committing the crime.

Joe Roberts took the stand for the prosecution and told them that we had indeed arrived at his flat, but that when he found out we had drugs, he asked us to leave. I thought he might have to tell the truth about his actual role because he was immune from prosecution, but he denied having any knowledge of the drugs before we had arrived at his house. It was never put to him that it was very strange that two men living in Holland, one of whom knew him well, would come to his house direct from the train station with so much drugs without his prior knowledge. He then revealed to the court that I had been to Wales a couple of months before. The prosecution used this fact to prove that I had come that time to set up the deal for December, which, of course, wasn't quite the case. It all seemed pre-planned to me.

David Jones, Joe's flatmate took the stand, but he was incoherent because of his alcohol problem. They did understand though that he had known me all his life and that the drugs, in his opinion, belonged to Ahmed. It had also seemed to him that I was working for Ahmed. He did not mention that Joe was supposed to sell it for Ahmed and that I was the middleman. Even though he was lying for Joe, he did his best to clarify that it was not my cocaine. This was, I expect, because we had known each other for so long, and he was doing his bit to help me.

Ahmed was led to the dock and swore on the Qur'an to tell the whole truth. It emerged that in his original statement Ahmed had told the police that I had lured him to come on a Christmas shopping holiday, without him knowing anything about the drugs. He alleged that I had sneaked the cocaine into his bag before we got on the bus to Ostend. Now he claimed that he knew about the drugs and that he had been working for me to bring a package to Wales that he thought was only hashish. His whole story was a lie. Throughout the proceedings, the evidence that I gave was confirmed by the prosecution.

When the judge summed up, he concluded that we had both lied throughout to save our own skins. My story had been confirmed and checked by the police who had travelled to Holland. Quite what I had said 'to save my own skin' baffled me, especially when I had stupidly stated that I was the one who was selling the coke when I was not. If I had told the truth about Joe, my part would have been accepted as courier and middleman, not supplier or distributor, which usually carries a tougher sentence. Covering up for Joe meant that I was actually admitting to a more serious role. All I could think of was that the police might have spoken to the judge about Joe working for them. Maybe this was the reason he knew that there were some lies involved.

A police prosecution witness took the stand and announced that the kilo of cocaine was worth an estimated street value of £1,485,000! I couldn't believe my ears. This was the most expensive kilo of cocaine in the whole world. Never before had there been such a high street estimate. I stand by the claim that this truly is a world record!

The logic behind this ridiculous over-estimate was entirely flawed. They claimed that one could sell a kilo of sugar, (2lb 2oz) with a dessert spoonful of cocaine added, for £50 pounds a gram. There are 1,000 grams in a kilo. They then reckoned that this 61 per cent pure cocaine could then be mixed with about thirty kilos of fine sugar, and sold for a total of £1,485,000. Cocaine has little commercial value when cut under 50 per cent. To try and sell such a drastic 'cut' – leaving it at '4 per cent' pure – to dealers that always tested it first would be suicide. Somehow the judge believed these ridiculous estimates. A desert spoonful of cocaine, costing say £150 – then mixed with a kilogram of castor sugar, could, according to the police, be sold on the street for £50,000! My barrister did not challenge it. Were they all in this together? It seemed that way. The judge, who was supposed to be up to speed with these things, believed that a kilo of cocaine could be sold for this extraordinary price. He didn't believe that my pay for this venture could only be about £4,000, half of which I had to pay back to the Turkish dealers. Therefore, in his mind the case was blown out of all proportion. He believed that it was a very costly venture involving large sums of money. The truth was that it only cost Ahmed about £20,000 for the kilo. (I believe he could have bought it for £16,000 but because he had organised so quickly an extra half-kilo at the last minute, he'd had to pay more.) I believe he borrowed half a kilo on top of what he bought himself. Ahmed was trying to sell it for £36,000 – that is, £1,000 an ounce.

The court was adjourned for lunch. All these facts and figures wouldn't matter to me now. The judge had retired to consider his verdict and I was certainly going to stay in jail for quite some time yet. When we came back after lunch the judge, Recorder Patrick Harrington QC, looked at us both sternly and pronounced that he had no alternative but to deliver harsh sentences and set an example to all drug dealers and smugglers.

'You are both hereby sentenced to twelve years on both counts of importing and supplying a class 'A' drug.'

That meant we got twenty-four years each, although these two sentences would run concurrently, meaning we would each serve only twelve years. I was looking at the judge through tunnel vision when he spoke those words. His eyes met mine and I could focus on nothing else, as if the whole room had gone blank except for his face. I was not going to show any emotion, so I stared directly at him and held my composure without flinching.

Ahmed was led away first and hit the door with his hand and shouted something out. I followed and banged the door too. The trial had taken four days. Sitting in the cell under the court afterwards made for a very sobering moment indeed. I wanted to curse God for this terrible sentence, but even there, I kept on thinking that he knew best, that somehow it would all turn out all right. An hour later I was on the way back to Swansea prison, and I kept saying to myself that I would not let this beat me. I prayed to God and asked for help with my appeal. Meanwhile, I found some compensation in the almost-immediate thought that I could use this time to get a better education. I had left school without any certificates, and, with some serious study perhaps I could even build a foundation for the life to come when I was released.

I got back to my cell, prepared to cry my eyes out, but strangely no tears came even though I was full of self-pity. 'Twelve years man!' I grumbled to myself. But quite surprisingly, it was not long before I perked up again. Somehow a peace came over me and I even began to believe that something really good could come out of it all. After about an hour, the Revd Lionel Hopkins, the new chaplain of Swansea prison, came to see me in my cell. He had been sent by the governor to see if I was all right. Instead of finding a broken man, he found one determined to turn this seeming misfortune into an opportunity to grow, and to use the time to his advantage. Lionel was a 'baby' prison chaplain (his own words) and was encouraged by such a positive attitude in these trying circumstances. No, I wasn't going to let this beat me. Though I felt terrible, deep down I knew that this could be the chance of a lifetime. It could make me or break me.

I knew too that if I tried it alone I would not succeed. But if the God who had created the universe was a part of it, then the opportunities were massive. Lionel handed me a New International Version of the Bible – from the Gideons – and signed it. For the next three weeks, I studied that Bible hard and it really lifted my spirits. It was the start of a much longer study. The next time I saw Revd Kerry Jenkins on the wing, I asked him to organise a Bible reading course for me.

After a couple weeks, I was called into the office and told that I would be transferred. I had the choice of Long Lartin or Dartmoor, so I asked which would be best for education? The officer told me that Long Lartin prison was a dangerous place, where there had been many stabbings.

'Dartmoor is probably the best for education Morris.'

I agreed to go to Dartmoor, even though this was the most notorious prison that I had ever heard about. Strangely, I was looking forward to my arrival there.

EIGHT

Secure within a mighty fortress

A two-hour drive from Swansea in a tiny sweatbox brought me to a small stop-over jail in Shepton Mallet where we stopped for lunch. I remembered my first visit to this Somerset town: it had been in 1970, when I'd travelled as a young hippy to the rock festival that later became Glastonbury. After a sandwich break of an hour and a half, we departed for 'Moor' in a bus with transparent plastic compartments. I looked out of the window at the many apple trees in the area and remembered the 'scrumpy' cider that we all drank many years before. That was the first time I had ever tasted it and right now I really fancied another gallon! I wasn't isolated in my own personal sweatbox this time, because of the see-through compartments, and so twenty of us prisoners could have a laugh and nervously encourage each other while anticipating our arrival at this notorious fortress prison.

It was raining when we reached Dartmoor, and visibility was very poor because of the low cloud, so I didn't get a good view of the place as we approached the entrance high up on the misty moor that day, 3rd October 1996. Built by American and French prisoners of war in the 1800s, the prison had a reputation and history that would make anyone shudder. But I was confident that God was with me, and I wondered about this prison and what would become of me there. As I said, I felt I could murder a drink, for old habits die hard, but apart from two little tastes of prison 'hooch' (home-brew made by inmates), I managed to stay clear the whole time I was there.

I was put in a cell on B-Wing. It had recently been renovated, and the sparkling orange linoleum floors of the cells impressed me (honestly, they were nice!). Lying on the bed a few days later, a picture – perhaps even a vision – came into my mind. I saw that I was speaking to a large crowd, which surprised me greatly. When I was about seven years old, I was asked to recite a poem at Holy Trinity chapel in Clydach, and I trembled from head to foot with fear. After that, I had always been very scared to speak in front of a group of people. I knew I was much too scared to do that. The picture clarified itself now. I saw myself speaking to a crowd in Kerry Jenkins' church in Clydach. No way, I thought – not me boy! And yet, in spite of my deep reservations I somehow felt that this picture had been given to me from above – planted in my mind even – and I had to do something about it.

Kerry sent me a Bible study course as requested. After I had completed this short series, there was no certificate to be gained. Perhaps, I wondered, the chaplain here would have some courses available. I was eager to know and understand what the Bible was really all about. So many people had their opinions, but they didn't really know; these days, opinions are considered more important than actual truth. Each time I read a verse in my Bible, I reasoned that knowing and understanding God's word would profit me more than anything else.

I couldn't wait for Sunday to come along, so that I could see the chapel and meet everyone. As soon as I got there, I was surprised to find only a handful of inmates attending. The Revd Bill Birdwood was the chaplain, and John

Coppin was his assistant. I had met Bill on the first day when he welcomed all new inmates at induction. There was no problem in getting to speak to them, and I asked John if there were any Bible courses that I could do. He got out some basic International Correspondence Institute (ICI) studies for me to choose from, and I picked out the first one: 'The Christian in His Community.' Well, my 'community' was a bit different from your normal community, but it was definitely a community nonetheless. This study challenged me to check my behaviour in ways that I hadn't before. I examined the way that I reacted to people when confronted with a negative situation. I even looked at the way I thought about people who disliked me or had hurt me. I soon realised that this all had to change. To learn all this took time, and even though I still sometimes snapped in a stressful situation – because my bad old self was fighting for dominance – my prayers seemed to give me much more control over my actions and emotions than ever before. A new self, aided and guided by the power of the Holy Spirit, took over. Sometimes this was very hard because my pride wanted desperately to settle scores, but I was undeniably changed.

I was moved onto D-Wing and after just two days was given the privileged job of kit store orderly. This was an answer to prayer. Just a week earlier I had asked God to give me a more enjoyable and rewarding job in this prison, instead of more cleaning. And now I had the choice of the best bed linen, blankets and clothes! To arrive on a wing and get one of the top jobs could have spelled trouble for me because others could have become jealous. But God was in control. I did the job well, and once again I was not harmed. Many inmates who had been hoping to get the job were very angry with me though. I felt that I was like Daniel in the den of lions (in the Bible, Daniel was thrown to the lions, but God miraculously protected him) and that God had shut up the mouths of the snarling beasts. Just like Daniel, I prayed morning, afternoon and night and all was well.

I applied for a transfer to HMP The Verne in Dorset, because I heard about the 'Kairos (Greek for "God's special time") Community Project', which was to be a Christian-run wing. A pilot scheme was going to start up there, and I was excited at the prospect of living at the heart of a Christian initiative. The excitement didn't last long though – the answer came back that I had been refused because I was not a C-cat (short for category) prisoner. An A-cat prisoner is considered high risk and they are housed in the most secure prisons in the country. B-cat prisoners have a little more freedom and security is slightly lower. C-cat prisoners live in semi-open conditions and are given a certain amount of trust to move about the prison. The Kairos project was only for C-cat prisoners, and I was considered a higher risk than that.

Learning and changing

Everyone goes with the flow in prison and to be different is to invite a lot of problems to head in your direction. Being a Christian in any situation – let alone in a prison – is a very brave step indeed because opposition abounds. People don't realise that behind everything to do with Christ, there are spiritual forces in the heavenly realms that do their best to tell our hearts that it's all a load of rubbish. The Bible states it (Ephesians 6:12) and I believe it! You will find that people do get angry or laugh when Jesus is mentioned and I have always wondered why. Now, here in prison, I knew that if I were to state that I had become a Buddhist or had converted to any other religion, no one would blink an eye, but when I spoke of being a Christian, it would stir up anger in others. Through my studies, I was beginning to understand that there are forces at work which are determined to lead all mankind away from the truth. That dragon in the Bible, the devil, walks about like a roaring lion, seeking someone to devour (1 Peter 5:8). That dragon, who had been chasing me for so long, never gives up. And it becomes even more of a battle when we become Christians.

I used to go along with the common assumption that the Bible has changed so many times that it bears no resemblance to the original. Now, through my studies, I see that this is simply not true! It really is just a common assumption. Many would affirm these false notions over and over, but they are wrong. I learned that all modern translations are carefully researched and approved by the best biblical scholars after years of hard translation from the original Hebrew and Greek texts.

My next Bible course was 'We Believe'. I wanted to understand exactly why I believed God, and therefore I also wanted to know more about him. When I first began to read the Bible I found it all too much – frightening even. I found everything from deep love to treachery and murder, sadness, heartache and pain. But then I found that there is a pattern running through it: God's love versus man's pride; truth versus lies; belief versus unbelief. And more important than all of that, the need to turn one's life around, to say sorry and to become reconciled with God through Jesus Christ. I began to understand how God could use men like Moses, King David, and St Paul, even though they were all murderers.

A week before Christmas 1996, I was asked by Deaconess Jo White to do one of the readings for the carol service. I was determined to conquer my old fear at last and trust in God's help. When the day arrived and we entered the chapel, I saw that it was full of guests from outside the prison. 'I can't go through with it,' I whispered to Jo when I passed her. She pleaded with me to do it, but I couldn't. The old fear had returned and was far too strong for me, and so someone else did the reading instead. After the service, I felt that I had let her down badly, but I was still determined to conquer the fear and to do it one day. That day came just a month later when I read the Sunday reading in front of fifteen inmates. I had trusted God to give me a bold spirit – which the Bible talks about – instead of a spirit of fear, which is from the devil. I even prayed as the moment came to go up to the front; I was determined to do it and to trust God.

I spoke too fast and my legs trembled, but I managed it – and I was really pleased that I had finally laid my public speaking fear to rest. From then on, by praying before I went up and remembering to speak more slowly, I got better as each week passed. Without God's help, I never would have attempted this; with it my fear had been conquered.

My helper on the kit-change job was Raymond Robson (Robbo). He was quite small in stature, but he was a very hard man with an explosive temper. He confided in me that he had noticed that I was different, and so I was able to share with him that I had given my life to God. He became very interested in knowing more, so I gave him a New Testament and suggested that he start by reading the Gospel of John. Every day he would come excitedly into my cell and share some new thing that he had discovered. I had been praying for a prayer partner and one day, I dared to ask him if he minded me saying a short prayer or two?

'No Brian,' he said. 'I'm not quite ready for that.'

But a couple of weeks later he came into my cell and asked me to pray about some news that he was waiting for. He had been trying desperately to contact his sister, asking her to visit him, but so far he had heard nothing. He thought that prayer – which I had raved about to him – might be the answer. I read a Bible verse, then spoke out a simple prayer, just asking for God's help, while Robbo was quiet. Three days later, Robbo burst into my cell.

'Brian, Brian!' he shrieked. 'It's amazing man, my sister finally wrote to me – she's coming to visit!' He was buzzing with excitement. 'The prayer has been answered.'

'God is good Robbo,' was my childlike reply.

'Yes Brian,' he laughed aloud, 'God is good!'

I reminded him again about the Scripture we had read before our prayer and he was amazed: 'Until now you have not asked for anything in my name. Ask and you will receive, and your joy will be complete.' (John 16:24)

Robbo just smiled and laughed. 'Praise the Lord,' he said.

My courses were really helping me to learn basic things about God, and were giving me a better understanding of the Bible, and this was why I had been able to help him.

I completed two more basic level Bible courses because I had so much time in my cell. These were 'Who Jesus Is' and 'Your Bible'. I got high grades, and the next time I sent the completed answer sheets to the ICI offices in Cheshire, they sent me back an intermediate course. This was 'Alive in Christ', and I passed again with high grades. I put my certificate on the wall next to the others.

All this time I had been waiting to hear about my appeal. I received some shattering news: the judge had refused me leave to appeal. I couldn't believe it. My solicitors warned me against pursuing it any further because it could result in me losing the time I had served. I felt devastated. 'What's your game Lord?' I questioned, but my studies helped me through this dark time. I knew I had to trust that God knew best, and that somehow it would work out in the end.

Since there was no hope of my appeal going any further I realised that I had to heed the warnings of my solicitors. I applied for repatriation to the Netherlands to serve the remainder of my sentence there. In any case, I knew it would take many months to get another hearing. The warning I received from my solicitors made me believe it was the only option open to me. Maybe in six months I could be on my way to Holland? I needed to see my son and Marie Claire. An information leaflet from the Dutch Embassy informed me that my case could be heard within six months, so this made me very hopeful that I would be successful. After all, I had lived in Holland for almost twenty-one years. I was now rather missing old 'cloggy land' and the carefree, no-fuss Dutch.

A supernatural high

We heard that a fifteen-strong team from a church in London – Holy Trinity Brompton – was planning to come to the prison for three days in April. This was excellent news. We only got to the chapel for forty-five minutes every week on a Sunday. Now we would get three afternoons together, praying and singing to God. Robbo was getting as excited as I was and he had picked up a copy in the chapel of a newspaper that HTB produced called *Alpha News*. He was amazed to read of the phenomenal growth of the Alpha course. The Alpha course is a series of talks and discussions which look at the claims of

Christianity. It was devised by HTB and was originally held there, but has now spread across the world.

On the first day of the team's visit, Robbo and I answered a call to go to the front for prayer. The next moment he was on the floor, flat out: knocked over by the power of God. We couldn't stop talking about it afterwards, and Robbo was now fully convinced that God was real. He told me about the strange sensation that he had experienced – it seemed like he had been filled with a liquid heat from his head to his toes; a cleansing heat. I wanted to experience the same and went forward on the next two days but nothing happened. I was very disappointed. I wondered why it was not happening to me. I thought that maybe God hadn't yet forgiven me for all my years of high living.

Off the back of HTB's visit, Chaplain Bill Birdwood decided to start an Alpha course and what was called a 'discipleship foundation' course (basically this was for people who had become Christians, and wanted to act more like Jesus, who lived a perfect life). Robbo signed up for Alpha, while I signed for both courses. I couldn't get enough.

Then I received what I thought to be wonderful news: I heard that I was eligible for repatriation. My Dutch residency permit had been checked out and I was free to apply. I knew it! I would be soon in Holland in an open prison doing easy bird. 'Praise the Lord!' I thought.

We were on a high after the Holy Trinity team's visit; even the officers had perked up. It seemed that holding prayer and worship in such a gloomy place had brought about an effect on all those who worked there. I applied to get into the education department, leaving the kit-change job. I was finding it too hard handling difficult prisoners who were never satisfied with the kit I gave them. It was a recipe for explosion. I was content to go back on cleaning until I was accepted on education. A cleaner is allowed out of his cell for most of the day while those who are not working are always locked up.

Our high didn't last for long. Suddenly there was a marked change in the way we were treated, and it felt to me that the devil was raging because of all the good that God had been doing. Even the cleaners were getting locked up more often. Now we were spending twenty hours of the day alone in our little cells. Often it was twenty-three hours a day, with prisoners only being let out to fetch meals.

Music hammered out all around, with House and Techno in the cell on the left, Pink Floyd in the cell on the right, Bob Marley above and The Fugees below. Inmates were constantly having conversations out of the window, some shouting from the fifth landing to the first. They swung home made 'lines' made from strips of bed sheets to pass on tobacco, rolling papers and other things. It was non-stop, head crippling noise that could turn many insane. I had my correspondence courses to finish so I kept myself busy all the time. I stuffed paper in my ears but it was never enough, and to make matters worse I was always cold, even in the summer. We were high up on the moor and the two-foot thick granite walls acted like a freezer. The four-inch heating pipe that passed through my cell into the next didn't do much to warm the place up. During study, one hand had to be tucked away to warm up; then after a period of time I would swap hands. Powerful lights shone through the high small window in my cell at night so there was never any real darkness for proper rest. I prayed for strength and God gave me the power to cope and I didn't lose heart. I was not as stressed as I could have been, although I was not perfect and occasionally snapped at some of the inmates.

I read story after story about what God had done in real people's lives. The chapel library had a large stock of Christian literature. These were real stories told by real people. I could not read the books that everyone else read from the regular prison library. They seemed to waste my precious time. I was determined that I would not to let this jail term have a negative effect on me. I realised that this was the best chance I would ever have to try and change my life. It would not be possible if I read too much fiction and crime stories like most inmates. With the many hours alone in that cell I continued to be amazed by what God had done in people's lives. The story of Jackie Pullinger, who was used by God to help many heroin addicts to real freedom, inspired me and brought tears to my eyes. People were miraculously healed in front of her eyes, through just faith and prayer, and this was incredibly exciting. I wanted God to use me in a similar way to how he used her, and I got down on my knees for long periods and pleaded with him that exactly that would happen, even in this prison.

The days and months went by and receiving letters brought some welcome comfort. My brother Chris wrote to me on a regular basis and so did Kerry, Claud, some of the Prison Fellowship volunteers and a few other friends. Kerry Jenkins enclosed stamps each time, which gave me so much help. I wrote at least ten letters a week and filled every line on both sides of the paper.

Another answer to our prayers was the arrival of John 'Finny' Finlinson at the Moor. Finding out that I had decided to follow God, he confided in me that he too was becoming a serious Christian. I encouraged him as much as I could and he not only joined our prayer group, but, having such a gentle character, he was used to bring many others along as well. We both played guitar and formed a worship band, often enjoying practice sessions in the chapel when many were locked up. We met and prayed with many of the authors of the life-story books we read. Doug Hartman, who wrote *King of the Conmen*, came to speak to us, as did Brian Greenaway, who wrote about his life as a Hell's Angel, and Chris Lambriano who was involved with the Kray brothers.

Then one day, Robbo, my first prayer partner and friend in the prison, and another inmate were suddenly taken off the wing. We were all confined to our cells, and a thorough search was started. Every cell was turned upside down. No one knew what was happening. Then we heard on the radio about a gun scare at Dartmoor. On the third day, a hand-made wooden pistol was found in the library on our wing. The rumour was that it looked like the real thing but it was only a solid piece of wood. We were locked up for a further four days and only let out for food two at a time. This took ages with over a hundred inmates on our so-called 'drug-free' D-Wing. The security officers came to question me about my friendship with Robbo and I told them the truth – that we usually talked about the Bible together, but it was obvious that they didn't believe me. The sterner they got, the firmer I stood. They thought there was much more to my friendship with Robbo. He had never mentioned a gun to me but he had told me about the many heavy beatings that had happened to inmates at Dartmoor. He had been a problem inmate for years and had never got on with any of the officers. He had spent nine years inside on this stretch, many of them in the punishment block for his resistance to the system's brutality. I still wonder if he went on in his

Christian journey; he had become a close friend of mine. I tried to contact him when I found out where he had been shipped out to, but I never heard from him again. Anyway, the security officers could find nothing to charge me with and left my cell.

Still, life wasn't getting any easier. Dave Ross, the inmate that I had a fight with in Swansea while on remand, arrived on the wing. His brother John was already in a cell opposite me but had not known about our fight. Now there was a potential recipe for something really bad to happen. Every time I walked passed him and caught his eye, he snarled and warned me I would be 'sorted' soon. They had five other friends who had arrived from other prisons – I knew because I'd met them all in Swansea. I now had to watch my back all the time. I prayed for these men and every time my temper swelled up, I got down on my knees and prayed for God to work on my heart and theirs. They didn't touch me, and I never reacted when provoked. That was a miracle for me. I was determined not to blow my chances of repatriation, and I continually put my trust in the Scripture, 'If God is for us, who can be against us?' (Romans 8:31).

Jonathan

I finally got a note from the education department saying that I could start there the following day. I was really glad to go off the wing because of the potential danger. I had attended an Alpha course in the chapel, the discipleship foundation course run in an office on C-Wing and completed four basic and four intermediate ICI Bible courses. I also passed a GCSE in English at the education department. I took a course with the gym officers on First Aid. The certificates were mounting up on my wall like wallpaper.

An inmate named Jonathan was finding prison very hard and couldn't cope well. He needed strong medication. He had been sent down to the punishment block for something trivial, and while there he attempted to hang himself from the light fittings. Fortunately, the makeshift rope that he used snapped, and he was brought back onto the wing, where the senior officer (SO) asked me to keep an eye on him. I went to his cell as often as I could to keep him company and to write his letters for him. He dictated a letter to his mother apologising for what he had done. It was really sad. He felt very low and couldn't snap out of his depression. One night I told him about Jesus, who would help him if he asked. There was no time to pray with him because association was finished and it was time for night lock-down. So I explained to him quickly how to pray and asked him to do it that night. The next morning he came down the stairs with a huge beaming smile on his face. 'Brian, I did what you told me to and I feel much better now.' He had given his life to Jesus.

Jonathan did well for seven weeks but then slipped back into depression. A kind officer opened my cell one day and asked if he could bring Jonathan down for some company. I thought it was a good idea. We were together all afternoon, during which time he told me that he was going to try and end his life again. I wanted to pray with him, but never got round to it because of many interruptions with inmates coming to the door. That evening during association I warned the SO that Jonathan might attempt to take his life again, but he told me that Jonathan was only trying to get attention. I pleaded with him to listen.

'Mr Passmore, he is serious. He's very confused – I've been with him all afternoon and I'm really worried about him. Please keep a close eye on him.'

Fifteen minutes after lock-down at eight, he cut his throat with a razor blade. He was rushed to the hospital wing, bandaged up and put on bed watch. The next morning he was found hanging by a rope made from some bed sheets he had ripped for this purpose. He had tied them to the high window, then stood on a table before kicking it away. This time, the rope didn't snap.

The SO looked very embarrassed when I saw him and went quickly into his office. I didn't see him after that for three weeks. He either took time off or was on holiday. I was very angry with myself afterwards that I didn't take the opportunity to pray with Jonathan when I had the chance. I believe the prayer that he spoke in his cell two months previously did not go unanswered. In my heart, I just knew God had used me to save tragic Jonathan's life. God knew how sick Jonathan was and I believe that they are together now.

Pain, lies, and more bad news

One day I received a letter from the Child Care Agency in The Hague. It was a copy of a warning to my probation officer that I had been very violent during Marie Claire's pregnancy. It seemed that Marie Claire was out to stop me getting repatriated to Holland, and was telling all these lies to the agency for that reason. I couldn't believe it. She had lied that I had threatened violence if she didn't agree to marry me, and also that I was very violent during her pregnancy. I was supposed to have written threatening letters demanding that she marry me. I did realise that because of her condition, my letters had been a bit too serious, but they had certainly not been threatening. Her grandmother had already written to me saying that Marie Claire wouldn't even read my letters.

It was a very hard blow to me to accept that because I was in prison, the social worker of the agency would believe her and send the report to my own probation officer. She had written it as if she believed it to be the truth. I felt like writing back and telling them what had really happened, but I felt God filling me with his peace and telling me to be patient. I realised that if I wrote a reactionary letter protesting my innocence, it would only go against me, but still it felt like a nail in the coffin. I knew that this was a ploy to stop me coming back to Holland and it hurt me deeply.

Now these accusations were a bitter pill to swallow, but I knew I must try to put it behind me. I realised that I could have done more to stop taking drugs myself and was as much to blame as she was. Deep down I still hoped that Marie Claire would write a sensible letter, and open up some kind of dialogue. There were so many things left unspoken.

In spite of this bitter disappointment, on 5th October 1997, I found the strength to give up smoking – after thirty-two years. I had prayed for this for a long time. Smoking is a real problem in prison. It is impossible to enjoy a cigarette on your own because inmates dive on you from all angles whispering 'two's up' (meaning you had to share). Running out of tobacco was agonising and constantly played on the mind. I asked God to take away my desire to smoke, and after four days of struggle, it became very easy and I lost the desire completely. I had tried many times in my life to stop but always started again because I couldn't stop gasping. Now there was no more gasping, and I had no craving at all. Again, this was answered prayer – a miracle!

The Holy Trinity Brompton team came again for three days and Bill Birdwood used the opportunity to hold a baptismal service. I had wanted to be baptised for some time, as I knew from my Bible that this was something that God required of me. There were about fifteen inmates waiting to be baptised. We all had a wonderful time, taking it in turns to be submerged underwater in the plastic pool used for the occasion. Just before we were baptised in the name of the Father, Son and Holy Spirit, each of us gave a public declaration of our faith in Jesus Christ and were given a personal verse from the Bible. Mine was from Philippians 4:19: 'And my God will meet all your needs according to his glorious riches in Christ Jesus.'

Then it was my turn to take the microphone. I was full of emotion and loudly stated: 'I now belong to Jesus and I want to serve him for the rest of my life,' to a thundering roar from everyone there.

We all sang at the top of our voices a hymn that had become our Dartmoor anthem: 'My Shackles Are Gone, My Spirit Is Free'. Some inmates cried openly with joy after being baptised and when we were all being taken back to our cells, one officer remarked,

'It's all an act just to get parole, you can't fool me!'

I was hurt by the comment, but kept my mouth shut, as did the others. We all just ignored him, and I don't think he was feeling so smug after that. He locked me back in my cell and I said, 'God bless you Mr Roof.' He just grunted in embarrassment.

Christmas came and went for the third time in prison. The Childcare Agency sent me a court report of my son's foster parent custody plan for the year. Reading that report, I discovered that Marie Claire had an additional name. Instead of Marie Claire Van Der Bosch, it was now Marie Claire 'Jansen' Van Der Bosch. That's how I found out that she was now married. It was a severe blow. It seemed that all I had hoped and prayed for was not God's plan and I'd had to learn the hard way. I had asked God many times to help me get over her, but I'd blindly walked in the wrong direction feeling a deep human need for her. Now I wanted to know God's will for my life and to stop getting it wrong every time.

I continued with my studies and prayer meetings, and never missed a chapel service. God knew better than I did. I believed in his word, the Bible, and I had to trust him. My cell was becoming overcrowded during our prayer times, so we split into two groups with Finny leading the other one. These were conducted at the end of association each night at five to eight when the screws opened our doors to get our flasks for water before lockdown. That meant there was a rush, but we had no other alternative. We asked many times for an official room to pray in, but were given no help. Some officers were really good though, opening our cells early. We were then able to pray longer, giving everyone a chance to say something out loud to God.

One day, an old officer named Goodwin decided to give me an official warning to 'Stop holding unauthorised Bible classes in my cell.' I prayed for him a lot after that and even though he tried so hard to catch me slipping up, he never did, though I'm sure he wanted to. He hated to think that we were con-artist inmates 'pretending to be religious' in order to get a lighter sentence. He had little to back him up. I had never been reported for any wrongdoing or bad behaviour since the fight in Swansea. I had studied hard and treated officers and inmates alike with respect. He was determined to bring me down but didn't have a chance – I was standing on the solid foundation and promises of Jesus Christ. Any hateful thoughts I had about him I brought up in my conversations with God, and asked for forgiveness.

I had completed ten intermediate ICI Bible courses, so decided to attempt college level. Because Kerry had told me of the complexity and depth of the book of Revelation, I decided that this would be my first course, mainly because it was the most difficult to understand. Kerry's 'Calvary Full Gospel Pentecostal Church' agreed to pay for it. I never found out who had paid for all the other courses I had finished. New ones just kept coming each time I completed them. I did well with the course 'Daniel and Revelation' and got 82 per cent, which gave me so much encouragement that I applied for funds from the 'Prisoners Education Trust', a charity to help prisoners study. They paid for the first of five modules for an advanced certificate as a 'Christian Communicator'.

The first course was 'Principles of Teaching'. The agreement was that if I did well, they would pay for the other four. With hard work, I managed to get an 'A' with a result of 93 per cent! I'd never expected to do so well; it was really good for my self-esteem. God was re-educating me. I completed the other four, which were 'Communicating Christ Cross-Culturally' (89 per cent), 'Principles of Journalism' (91 per cent), 'Principles of Preaching' (85 per cent), and 'How to Speak in Public' (83 per cent). That last result was a real laugh, considering how terrified I used to be of public speaking.

The news came in August 1998 that the Dutch had refused to repatriate me because my circumstances were not serious enough, and my sentence was too severe. I wondered what circumstances could be more serious than a man separated from his son and the country in which he'd lived for twenty-one years. It was another devastating blow. It had taken eighteen months for this news to finally arrive. When it had been passed by the British side after a year, I'd really though that I was home and dry. Now I had no appeal and would probably have to do eight years in prison (two-thirds was the norm and I had a 12-year sentence). I was sick! 'What are you up to Lord?' I complained. I went back to my cell feeling like giving up this Christian lark. Deep in my heart I knew that God had his reasons, hard though it was to accept. I opened my Bible and my eyes fell upon this verse: 'Many are the plans in a man's heart, but it is the Lord's purpose that prevails' (Proverbs 19:21). I felt that it was a direct message from God to me. I was comforted, and knew that I must go on trusting him.

Confessions

That same day, during Saturday afternoon association, Finny asked me if he could bring an inmate who wanted to become a Christian. Still wrapped up in my own troubles, I was about to turn him away when I thought, 'You may regret this for the rest of your life.'

I decided to let him in. Jamie was a huge man with a boxer's nose, in for violent armed robbery. He looked embarrassed but I reassured him that this would be the best decision of his life. I explained that I'd almost turned him away because of the bad news I had received only two hours before. Finny asked me to pray but I couldn't. I asked Finny to do it. Jamie repeated a prayer of confession after Finny and once I'd heard that, my own problem seemed irrelevant. A man had just been 'saved' in my cell and all heaven was rejoicing (Luke 15:7). How could I complain? The fact that this great thing had happened on the day that I got the worst news possible was surely not coincidental. I realised again that God had a plan for my life, and remembered a verse I had read recently in my Bible: 'For I know the plans I have for you, declares the Lord, plans to prosper you and not to harm you, plans to give you hope and a future' (Jeremiah 29:11).

Soon after this, Finny decided to confess to other crimes that he had committed. The Holy Spirit, who was now working inside him, had convinced him to do this after he read 1 John 1:9: 'If we confess our sins, he is faithful and just and will forgive us our sins and purify us from all unrighteousness.' He was making a brave move and I admired his faith.

I decided to follow his example, and contacted a solicitor in Plymouth, who was the nearest to Dartmoor, to make fresh statements. This time I told the truth about Joe's involvement in the crime, because the more he ignored me, the more I became convinced that he had been working with the police. After making the new statement, I hoped that I could prove an injustice. I believed that the police should have disclosed their use of Joe to entice me to come over with the drugs. I gave all the letters from Joe that I had kept to the solicitor and told him that if Ricky or Joe had telephoned the customs in Dover, it would be on record; even the police would be required to keep a record of Joe's involvement. This could be a case of entrapment, I thought. I felt that I had no alternative than to make this statement; it was the only option open to me. It was not betrayal or revenge – Joe would be immune from prosecution and I would discover the truth. To show my sincerity, I admitted in my statement that I had dealt in drugs before and mentioned a few of the crimes revealed in the first few chapters of this book. I had not given this information to the police and I realised that all that I wrote in my new statement would be heard in court and could go heavily against me. This time I was telling the whole truth, and I believed in my heart that God would honour my honesty. I left it with the solicitor and realised that I had taken a big step.

Christmas passed again, and I applied for a transfer to Maidstone in Kent. I received news a couple of months later that I had been accepted. I'd been keen to move there because it was nearer for those who might be visiting me from Holland. There was a swimming pool there too. But even in such a remote spot as Dartmoor, there had been those who had visited me. Joshua, my Dutch friend from my drinking and snorting days in the Ned Kelly Café, finally found me after tracking me unsuccessfully for a year. He came as soon as he could to visit me. It was great to see him again.

I received more visits. Revd Kerry Jenkins had been twice to Dartmoor and my brothers John and Raymond had come with their wives Angela and Anneke. My two Scottish mates Jim and Big Andy, who I had met in Holland, had come at different times too. The Prison Fellowship also visited me and I was very grateful to Ann and Margaret, Jane, Roz and Hazel. They were all such wonderful Christians who encouraged me so much with their letters too. God did not leave me without friends. True, many of the old, so-called friends disappeared from my life after my arrest, but I had gained a whole bunch of solid, encouraging fellow Christians instead.

It was now two years and three months since my arrival at HMP Dartmoor. I was sitting an exam in the chaplain's office when an officer interrupted and announced:

'Morris RX1112! I've got good news and bad news for you. First the bad news: you are not going to Maidstone B-cat.'

My heart sank, but not for long as he continued:

'But you can go to Highpoint C-cat in Suffolk tomorrow if you wish. It's near Harwich for your visits from Holland.'

I felt like jumping up and giving him a hug, but I checked myself and calmly accepted his proposal. I couldn't wait to get out of the place.

I was really excited now to be leaving 'Darkmoor' B-cat and to be going to a C-cat prison. It had certainly been a hard learning ground, but we had shared many prayers there and I had managed to progress quite a way on my Christian journey because of it. I would certainly miss the chaplaincy team a lot, not to mention our prayer group, which had grown and kept steady even when many left. Finny was doing a wonderful job co-ordinating the whole thing, and he faithfully prayed for an official room to meet for prayer. The chapel numbers were up to an average of fifty each week and I felt that God had answered my prayers – that he would do big things at Dartmoor.

Kerry, Finny and I had prayed together once in the spare chapel room that this 'fortress of doom' would become a 'citadel of light' for a Christian revival in Britain's prisons. I knew that God had used me well in his plans at Dartmoor. Many Christians pray often for the prisons and Dartmoor seemed to receive prayers from around the whole country. God is changing Dartmoor steadily in his own time. It is a place I will never forget. The real miracle for me was that God had brought me through the Dartmoor experience without getting put on report once for bad behaviour. I had passed all my urine tests for possible drug or alcohol use. I had not answered back to an officer in all that time. I had not got into any fights. So many inmates got put on report, 'charged' in front of the governor and sent down to the punishment block for the most trivial of reasons. God was obviously doing deeper things in me.

So it was goodbye HMP Dartmoor, and hello Highpoint. What plans did God have for me there? I was soon to find out.

NINE

Highpoint of jail

It was February 1999 when I left Dartmoor Prison, to set out on a six-hour journey to HMP Highpoint, near Newmarket in Suffolk. Some still called it 'Knifepoint' because of the many stabbings that once took place there. We got to the reception at five past six and the senior officer there was just going home.

'Sorry,' he moaned. 'I can't get you onto the wing until tomorrow morning.' 'I'll have to put you down in the block for the night.'

The 'block' was the punishment area. I felt like protesting, but instead I meekly replied that this was no problem. I'd begun to reason, and even to feel in my heart, that every hurdle I now encountered must all be part of God's plan.

I was welcomed inside by the stern 'block screw' with these words:

'Dinner finished half an hour ago.'

I was starving! But fair play, he managed to scrape up a chicken Kiev, a bag of Coco Pops, some milk and a tea-kit with a flask of hot water, for which I was very grateful. Then I was locked in a filthy cell, complete with mattress on the floor and stylish cardboard furniture. Even there I thanked God, for I now had the faith to believe that I must be there for a reason. As soon as I sat down, a voice from the left cell pleaded with me to give him a 'burn'.

'Sorry,' I replied, 'but I stopped smoking eighteen months ago.' I didn't hear much from him after that.

As the night wore on I got talking through the heating pipe hole in the cell on the right to a black Londoner named Wolfie. As we talked, he told me that he had been kicked off the 'Kairos' wing for some problem or other. Then it came back to me. Two years before I had prayed to get on the pilot Kairos Christian initiative wing in HMP The Verne. I had forgotten about it, but God had not. I had no idea that there was another Kairos wing, especially at Highpoint, but it was true, although they had only started this project six months previously. Here was an answer to a prayer that I had forgotten all about.

Wolfie asked if I could explain something about the book of Revelation that he didn't understand. Because I had completed a college course on the subject at Dartmoor, I was able to answer most of his questions. I had kept a New Testament in my back pocket. I had been searched before they locked me up and was not allowed anything in these punishment cells, but somehow they had missed it. As the night wore on, Wolfie asked me to pray for him. Now I was praying for someone through a pipe, and I never ever saw the man face to face! I knew for sure that God had sent me there. It was a very strong confirmation that I would have been foolish to deny.

Does God exist? I cannot conduct a scientific experiment and prove that he does, but I know that I have prayed from my heart and God has answered, just as is promised in the Bible, in Jeremiah 29:13: 'You will seek me and find me when you seek me with all your heart.'

I was beginning to understand that God made us as individuals and loves each one of us dearly. I read Psalm 139

– which talks of how God 'knitted me together in my mother's womb' – and realised how well he knew me.

I arrived on the induction wing the next morning feeling brilliant. I was on a high. The day seemed to have God's stamp on it. I felt so at ease, as if I had a blanket of peacefulness wrapped around me. I was put in a cell with a young lad of about twenty-two, and we got on well enough. At the induction meeting for newly arrived inmates I mentioned my interest in the Kairos Community Project and told the SO about my Bible studies. Normally, you were required to fill in an application form and had to wait at least three weeks to get on Kairos, but I was fast-tracked onto the wing in four days. Again, I felt that God was confirming that he wanted me there.

I applied for a gardening job. The three years, two months I had being shut up in Swansea, Bullingdon and Dartmoor had given me a longing to have some sun on my face. Again, things happened quickly here and I was soon accepted for a job on the gardens. I felt absolutely wonderful when I was out in a field on my own with no officers in sight. I discovered that there was a massive increase in freedom between a B- and C-category prison.

On the Kairos wing, it seemed that no one was really serious about Jesus apart from Dennis, a man from Bedford. He worked on the gardens with me and we were able to discuss many Bible topics. We both worked hard and got on well together, and I encouraged him to start a Bible class on the wing. It seemed like most of the lads there had only come onto the Kairos wing to get a better ride within the system. I asked Dennis to pray with me and he was happy to. After that, we prayed regularly every day. Before long, another inmate joined us. Our Bible class was advertised on the notice board by the warder's office. Soon, between five and ten inmates were turning up each week.

Dennis had studied the Bible extensively in the three years he had been inside. He was a bit of a loner there but was an excellent teacher. (He was also an artist and painted the walls of our Kairos meeting and TV room with a mural showing inmates continually re-offending and going back to prison in an ongoing vicious circle.) His confidence as a Bible student enabled him to take the lead in teaching. I learned many things from the studies which he took us through, but most of all I learned that God does not abandon men who have faith (see Hebrews chapter 11).

An orderly cue

The food at Highpoint was excellent compared to that at Dartmoor. The chicken Kiev that I had received down the block was regularly served on the wing, and it was excellent. In Dartmoor, we got them only on Bank Holidays and at Christmas as a special treat. There was hardly any 'lock-down' with long periods in our cells like we experienced at the Moor. And I was getting quite fit now, working outside in the garden and going regularly to the gym; I had gained some colour in my cheeks for the first time in years. Highpoint was a big relief for me, but many inmates there never stopped complaining. They thought the food was no good, that there was too much lockdown and not enough things to do. I thought it was paradise after Dartmoor!

The chapel was much larger than Dartmoor's. The Revd Mark Hunt was the head chaplain and Stewart Beaumont was his assistant. They were both gentle guys, revved up by the chance to do God's work. Six weeks after I arrived, the chapel orderly, Dave, told me that the chaplaincy team had put me on the top of the list to take over his job when he was released in the near future. Then one day Mark Hunt came to my cell to talk and pray with me because I was missing Marie Claire and Sonny so much. He helped me to see that it was about time I put it all behind me and accepted that God had settled that matter. After we prayed, I asked Mark if it was true he wanted me as his orderly. He confirmed that the job was mine if I wanted it, and this made me feel wanted and special. I had wanted the chapel orderly job at Dartmoor, but realised in hindsight that I had not been ready then. Now I had the chance of learning first-hand how to connect hurting people with Jesus Christ. What a privilege! Me – chosen by the chaplaincy team! Could this have been God's reward for my faithfulness in Dartmoor? There in my prison cell I cried tears of joy. I felt happier than I had in ages. I thanked God over and over.

I realised that this job would require certain controlled behaviour, and that if I did not focus on becoming an even more disciplined person, I would soon lose it. It was a wonderful opportunity to be given this job. The chapel was large with a long corridor full of side rooms used as offices and meeting places. I had my own kitchen there, where I made the tea and coffee with which I welcomed every inmate who came to visit. It was mostly hurting inmates that came to see the chaplain. I was the first person they saw as they came into the chapel, so I did my best to make them feel as welcome as possible. I realised that I also had an important role to play in their visits.

I soon learned that a little love goes a long way when people are hurting. I also began to realise that the way things looked could have a positive, welcoming effect on those that came to see the chaplain. So I polished the woodwork and kept the place spotless. I washed the chaplain's robes and ironed them neatly. And I made sure that when I served a hot drink, it was properly hot, even if there were a hundred or more to serve. I took real pride in the job. One of my tasks was to put out all the tables, chairs and toys for the children's visits. This was a unique opportunity for inmates to receive their wives and children in a more relaxed atmosphere. The usual noise of the packed visiting hall could often be very stressful for both the children and parents. This chapel visit service was sponsored by a charity and I volunteered to help it run smoothly by setting everything up and cleaning it all afterwards. I loved working in the chapel.

A few grumbling inmates were angry with me because they felt I had been given 'their' job, but I explained to them that no one could claim such a position. Only God chooses his workers, and I really did feel that I was chosen for the job. There was a library so full of Christian books that we hardly had room for them. Also, I was allowed to use the chaplain's shower. It was a high-powered affair and it was the most special treat and privilege. On our wing the showers were dirty and always occupied. Here I could take a shower at leisure. It was simply the best job in Highpoint! I had earned £5 per week in Dartmoor but now I received £12. Suddenly I was rich too!

Mark, the prison chaplain, called me to his office. He asked me if there was any pressing matter that he could help me with. I told him that I wanted to contact my long lost daughter Erika. She was born in 1973 and was the daughter of Maria, the girl who I'd met on holiday in Cornwall and hooked up with again in London. Maria became pregnant with my child, but declined when I asked her to marry me because she knew that we didn't love each other. I had moved back to Wales just after, and only ever saw two brief glimpses of Erika before her mother and I drifted out of contact.

Mark phoned the social security in Penzance, Cornwall for me but couldn't get through. I had received a letter from this office in 1979 when I was living in The Hague. I am sure it must have been about child maintenance, but I had never written back. Mark was very gentle with me as we dealt with this, because it was a real raw spot, and so I felt at ease with him. He had been a pastor in India and China and had travelled extensively throughout South East Asia. I had a few things in common with him and we often shared our experiences together. Later I contacted the Salvation Army to see if they could find Erika for me, but they wrote back saying that it was too late. They said that it might end up upsetting any new family that she may have. I believed that they were right so I decided to leave it with God.

A friend of mine on the wing, called Dave, wanted to renew his marriage vows in a church. His wife Anne was in the women's prison across the road. It took a while for Mark Hunt to set up but it was all arranged and the big day arrived. Then an officer with a very cocky attitude came and told Dave mockingly that it had been called off. At first, Dave was devastated. He had been looking forward to being with Anne and saying their vows for the first time in a church. He almost lost his temper with the officer but God must have helped him, for he was able to take a deep breath and calm himself. He was still angry with the officer when he came to tell me about it and I did my best to console him.

'Let's see what God can do.' I suggested, 'After all, he is able to do things that seem impossible.'

I turned to the Bible, to Matthew 18:19 and read to Dave: 'If two of you on earth agree about anything you ask for, it will be done for you by my Father in heaven.'

Then I asked Dave, 'Do you believe in God's promise?'
'Yes,' he answered.

Then we prayed about it, giving thanks for God's word. An hour later Dave came to my cell and told me that the service was back on. Dave met Anne in the chapel and they renewed their vows. I was chapel orderly so it meant I could share the moment with them. This was a great boost to faith for Dave and myself, and yet more proof that God answers prayer.

In the summer of 1999, a few months after I had come to Highpoint, I was feeling a bit down at the thought that I would still be inside for at least four more years. I had been in since December 1995, and there seemed to be no hope of getting out earlier than December 2003. That was until I received a letter from my new solicitors in Plymouth stating that Ahmed Polonov, my co-defendant, had seen his sentence reduced by two years in January 1999. It was now June, and this was the first I had heard of it. He must have failed with his original appeal, and it had taken him over three years to get a successful hearing. I had abandoned my appeal to try and get repatriated to Holland to be near my son and Marie Claire. Now I knew for sure that I had good grounds to re-open my appeal and, more importantly, that I would probably get two years knocked off my sentence too. An inmate named Alan in the opposite cell from me studied the law books and found that there was now a disparity in the sentences. It could not remain that way, especially when I had pleaded guilty at the earliest opportunity and Ahmed had not. Things were looking up.

Changing times, changing lives

There was no Alpha Course at this prison, but I asked Mark Hunt if we could have one. He revealed that he had been thinking about starting a course for some time, and before long it was up and running. When the Alpha initiators from Holy Trinity Brompton turned up to open the course they were very surprised to see me again. I'd had the pleasure of experiencing seven of their three-day visits to Dartmoor, and they knew my face well, especially as I had completed three Alpha courses there. Now I was able to complete and work on three more at Highpoint.

The Kairos 'weekend' arrived. This was an intense Christian learning experience, part of the Kairos initiative for all of us on this wing, and although it was called a weekend, it actually went on for four days. Priests, vicars, pastors, lay preachers and other volunteers, about fifteen in all, gave seminars and told their stories. The twenty-four inmates were split up into four groups of six. Each group had two of the Kairos team helping on their table. After each seminar, we were required to make a drawing about what we had learned. Then each group was asked to stand before everyone and give a short explanation about their drawing. This was great fun, seeing inmates – some shy, some brave – giving these amusing explanations.

During the four days, the tables at which each group sat were filled with sweets, cakes and drinks. Cards of encouragement from all around the world, from different Kairos initiatives, schools and churches, were read out and hung on the walls around. It was a very touching experience. There was also provision for all the inmates, visitors and chaplaincy team to eat together in the dining hall. The usual procedure was that we would eat in our cells, in which we were locked after we had fetched our food from the wing servery. They had brought in some special dessert treats as well. By the end of the four days, everyone had put on several pounds!

As it did come to an end, there was a presentation ceremony where each of us was presented with a Kairos cross. We were led into the chapel to thunderous applause. It was full of local dignitaries and even representatives from the Home Office, all singing 'When the saints go marching in'.

The altar was cleared for the twenty-four of us to sit in front of everyone. Each inmate got an opportunity to speak about what being on the Kairos programme had meant, and also about how God had helped them. There were some very moving speeches, and also a few hilarious ones. At the end, an inmate who had been part of the last Kairos weekend – Dennis our ex Bible class teacher – gave a closing speech.

The 'Next Step Programme' is a follow on from the Kairos weekend. Its aim is to develop, over a substantial period, the ideas that the Kairos weekend introduced. These ideas are then presented in weekly seminars by trained staff. Some of the topics covered were: forgiveness, self-centred love, others-centred love, prayer, acceptance of self, acceptance of others, and how to change.

I also finished the college course on 'How to Speak in Public' and ordered the final one – 'Principles of Journalism' – for the certificate entitled 'Christian Communicator'. At around the same time I started a creative writing course with Exeter University called 'Write Away'. I also decided to become a 'Listener.' This was a branch of the Samaritans, which they co-ordinated in prisons. Many lives have been saved after someone 'listened' to them. I passed the six-week training course and had to be ready to be called on at any time. I was called down to the punishment block to listen to suicidal inmates pouring out their problems. Some just wanted to use the listeners to bring them drugs, but generally listeners would not tolerate this and left quickly. When inmates asked us to bring drugs, we wouldn't give them away to the guards. We just took our leave and made some excuse to the guards about why we left so early.

After completing 'Principles of Journalism', I received my advanced certificate. I was so proud to receive an academic recognition and wished my mother were alive to see it. I then decided to do the five modules of the 'Christian Counsellor' series to follow on, which would take about a year of study by correspondence. They were modular goals on the way to an American BA degree. I paid for two courses myself, after saving from my £12 weekly wages. Pastor Kerry's church in my hometown of Clydach paid for two and Claud Trigger, my old counsellor friend who I'd found through *Challenge* magazine, paid for one. I had many people praying for me, but they also helped me out in practical ways too.

Looking up

There was a brand new 'Enhanced Regime' called South Five Wing, which I was entitled to go on. It had the most modern of cells, complete with TV, and it was a very tempting proposal. However, because I knew that God had brought me onto the Kairos Wing, I decided to stay there as long as possible. By this time, Dennis had left for a D-category open prison, so I prayed, asking God to send a mature companion for me to learn from.

Three weeks later, Danny Lloyd arrived. He was 52, about five-foot-ten, and balding, with glasses. I knew straight away that he was the answer to my prayer. We became very close and soon got down to starting a prayer group again. Even if other inmates didn't turn up, it didn't matter to us: Danny always came and we encouraged each other through prayer and reading God's word. He had studied ICI College courses just like me, but many years earlier. I was able to learn and mature a step further, thanks to his excellent leadership and help.

I wrote regularly to Finny in Dartmoor and encouraged him to apply for a transfer to Highpoint. He wrote that he was still waiting, but meanwhile prayer had been answered. They had been given a room to pray in officially. It was a big breakthrough in Dartmoor, where little change occurred. Finny had to wait a while longer before he was allowed to come. It was great to see him eventually, a year after I'd left Dartmoor. He joined our prayer group, bringing his wonderful faith and ability to encourage with him.

My brother Raymond and his wife Anneke came from Holland to visit and brought me some new clothes. It was great to see them again. They didn't have so far to travel this time, as HMP Highpoint was only fifty miles from Harwich. The new cross channel SeaCat, a four-hour service, was much faster than the old ferries that I had so often travelled on. After the visit they went to Wales for a week and then came again to see me on the way home. They were glad that it was going so well for me at Highpoint.

One of my chapel duties was to put out the chairs for the Thursday night Christian meeting. I arranged them in a big circle, usually putting out twenty chairs. In the afternoon, I would stand in the middle of the circle of chairs and pray that God would make it a good meeting. I decided to see if God would answer some prayers so that I could use this to encourage the inmates. Each week I increased the number of chairs by one or two and prayed for each one to be filled, but with no more people than the amount of chairs set out. I didn't know beforehand how many inmates would turn up from the wings. Often one or two wings would be on lock-down due to shortage of staff, so those inmates could not attend. There were about ten wings at Highpoint. I also didn't know how many outside visitors would arrive.

Gradually, week by week, I pushed the number of chairs up until I reached forty. Incredibly, not one chair was ever empty and not one extra was ever needed: every time they were filled exactly. I did this for about twelve weeks, and it was amazing to see this miracle over and over and the excitement that it caused. Many lads came to believe as a result of this.

Bad advice

Meanwhile, because I had given another statement with new information to my new solicitors in Plymouth, the advice they received from counsel was forwarded to me. I quote from the transcript:

ADVICE

In this case I am asked to advise Mr Morris as to whether grounds exist for him to apply for leave to appeal against conviction and sentence, or for his case to be referred to the Criminal Cases Review Committee. Mr Morris pleaded guilty at Swansea Crown Court to one offence of Fraudulent Evasion of the Prohibition on the Importation of Cocaine and one offence of Possession of Cocaine with Intent to Supply. On 19th September 1996, Mr Morris was sentenced to a total of 12-years imprisonment.

The basic facts are not in dispute. Mr Morris and his co-defendant did import approximately one kilogram of cocaine into this country from Holland where he, Mr Morris had been living for many years. Having arrived in Swansea, they had sold approximately one ounce of the drug prior to the police raiding their hotel room on 17th December 1995 and seizing the cocaine and equipment used for weighing it out and testing its purity. Throughout the proceedings, Mr Morris made no mention of the part played by Mr Joe Roberts. Mr Morris has now given instructions to the effect that this importation was at the request of Mr Roberts and that Mr Roberts 'had the means of moving the cocaine on'. All Mr Morris said to the police at the time was that he and his co-defendant had visited Mr Roberts on his arrival in Swansea, but did not implicate him in the crime. It is Mr Morris's belief that Mr Roberts informed on them. The first question therefore is whether, if it can be established that Mr Roberts was indeed both the instigator of the offence and the informant, that would entitle Mr Morris to have his conviction overturned. I regret to say that the answer is no. This is because English Law is settled and quite clear on this point.

After citing a 'number of cases of the court's strong disapproval of the use of *agents provocateurs* to induce people to commit crimes, which they would not otherwise have committed,' he went on to say:

In Mr Morris's case, there is no suggestion that the whole enterprise was tainted from the outset in the sense that Mr Roberts was acting as an agent of the police in promoting the importation. Rather, the highest it could be put against Mr Roberts is that he informed on Mr Morris and his co-defendant out of fear of police investigation into his own activities, he being afraid that the police would link them to him after their visit to their address. In any event, Mr Morris and his co-defendant sold a quantity of the cocaine they had imported without any assistance from Mr Roberts. It could not therefore be argued that no crime would have been committed without Mr Roberts's involvement. I therefore have to advise Mr Morris that I do not see any realistic chance of him succeeding in any appeal against his conviction.

This hit me hard, and it all began to churn over again in my mind. I knew that the statement that Ahmed and I had sold a quantity of the drug without the assistance of Joe Roberts could be disproved because there was evidence that we had arrived from the station on the first day by taxi. I had sent Ahmed to Joe's house by taxi while I was suffering from cold turkey. The police had found a note in the hotel room that I had given Ahmed to help him find the Three Compasses pub, which was two doors away from Joe's house. The taxi driver confirmed the journey from Swansea to Clydach in his police interview. Joe's flatmate David and wheeler-dealer Ricky knew that Joe was involved. There was another witness named Jason who had also seen me at Joe's because he had helped me by giving me some methadone. There were also the two men that had brought Ahmed back to the hotel from Joe's. They had waited outside while I got out of bed to get the coke from the stash upstairs for Ahmed to weigh out. Joe had telephoned me in Holland from Clydach to encourage me to bring drugs. I don't know where he phoned from but I would guess it was from the phone box near where he lived. Would there be any calls on record to my flat from this box near Joe's? I was not sure if the records survive that long.

As I write this now, I still have many questions left unanswered. It would be nice if Joe came and spoke openly with me. After all, I did try to protect him. I have no bitterness towards Joe or Ricky – I wish them well and only pray that they too might discover the mighty changing power of Jesus Christ. But, for my part, I have been completely honest and have put everything right before God.

Rays of light

As chapel orderly, I was kept very busy each week, making tea and coffee and dishing out the cakes that Mark Hunt bought for the Alpha course. The discussion groups were lively and interesting. Some disbelieving inmates would argue their point, determined to prove that all this Jesus stuff was nonsense. I saw some of these men mellow over the weeks and eventually even give their lives to God. They had taken time to enquire and research the facts, and had not only become convinced, but had surrendered to Christ as well. It was amazing to see.

I was concerned to see inmates get involved in regular meetings, Bible study and prayer. I knew they were likely to fall back into their old ways because I knew only too well that remaining on the road and staying a committed Christian is very hard. To see the rich transformation of the lives of those who did was truly wonderful to behold. I have seen angry inmates who had committed terrible crimes, kneeling down with us and praying for forgiveness, and I know that this is not something for wimps. It takes a real man to face up to the fact that he alone is responsible for his choices in life.

The next Kairos weekend came up and I was asked by the co-ordinators if I would like to do the closing speech. An inmate who'd been on the previous weekend was usually asked to do this. It was an honour to be asked, and even though I was still afraid of public speaking, I accepted.

I had been on the Kairos Wing for eleven months, and I felt that it was time to accept my invitation to South Five Wing, because it had become far too noisy for me to study where I was. Most of the Kairos weekend group that I had been part of had gone on to live in the enhanced wing or had been released. There were only a few of us left. When I left, some inmates accused me of being a deserter, but that didn't bother me because I knew that it was God's time for me to move on.

South Five was the most comfortable wing that I had ever been on. It must have been one of the best in the country: efficiently run by a PA system controlled from the central office, which was so much easier for both the officers and inmates. Even fresh toast and jam was available every evening. There were regular urine tests, but if you stuck to the rules and stayed drug free, this was a place of relative luxury. The rules were there for our own good; any that were broken brought swift justice, with inmates who did so being sent to the basic wing or 'the block' on the same day.

So many inmates found it so hard to stop taking drugs, and no matter how crafty they were, they all eventually got caught. It's a humiliating experience for them when they are taken off the wing that they hoped for so long to get on. There were three 'Regimes' in prison. 'Enhanced,' 'Standard,' and 'Basic'. It was quite a drop in privileges to be sent to Basic, and it took a long time to get back up the levels. Many never did, because when all the not-so-disciplined inmates were put together, the Basic regime became a breeding ground for even more trouble. That's why it's so important for prisoners to receive encouragement and love – to lift them out of their self-perpetuating downward spiral.

Mickey Slater, who was serving life, was also studying Bible courses, and joined me for prayer each day. South Five Wing was a building with a path right around it, and the main doors to the building were open during association. To keep fit, and to catch the occasional ray of sun, I started running around the path every day. After running, I would walk with Mickey, who was excellent company. He became a faithful prayer partner, always turning up at my cell at exactly the same time each evening.

Danny Lloyd also came off Kairos and joined us on the wing. We spent our association time walking round and round the South Five building, talking for hours. Danny was a special man, full of loving kindness, and was always a pleasure to be with. He was an ever-present help to any inmates who just needed to talk; he had a wonderful patience and maturity that everybody loved. We met for prayer every weekday evening in my cell, because it was nice and quiet on the end of the wing. Our prayer group was now three-strong, and meanwhile Finny continued the prayer group on the Kairos Wing.

Later Philip, a Dutch citizen from Ghana, joined us as well. A wonderful man who was deeply sorry for his crime (cocaine smuggling), he was a Christian who had struggled and then fallen, but who had realised the error of his ways and returned to his faith. He told me that he believed that God allowed everything to happen to him because his church in Holland had become too complacent. They had forgotten about those who really needed help. Philip believed that God brought him into prison to humble him and teach him a fundamental basic truth to bring back to his church.

I don't believe that God is watching us with a big stick ready to hit us when we do wrong, but I do believe that he will allow situations to overtake us in order that we might be brought to a level of spiritual maturity where he can use us better. Philip had excellent teaching qualities. His father was a pastor in Ghana and I was sure he would follow his example and become an excellent pastor one day. He carefully prepared Bible studies for our prayer meetings. Listening to him explaining what the Bible meant showed that he had prepared thoroughly for these meetings. I'm afraid I wasn't as thorough as Philip was when it was my turn.

Now we had four men regularly praying and studying the Bible. Our prayer time was a source of strength to us all on the wing. The officers admired our efforts and dedication and offered us an official room to pray in, which was yet another amazing answer to prayer. They even made posters and hung them up for us to attract others to our prayer group. The South Five officers wanted this wing to be the best, and they had noticed how well disciplined we were and wanted other inmates to take note. I am sure that's the reason they helped us develop our prayer group. Many others joined us too!

Reasons to be cheerful

It was at this time that I received a letter from the Criminal Office. This is what was written:

> The Appellant having been convicted in the Crown Court at Swansea on the 7th June 1996, was sentenced on the 19th September 1996 to a total sentence of 12 years imprisonment.
>
> THE COURT OF APPEAL CRIMINAL DIVISION on the 9th November 1999 CONSIDERED the application to treat the notice of abandonment as a nullity.
>
> AND HAS Granted the application.

This was brilliant news and meant that I could finally proceed with the appeal. The full truth would not come out now, but at least I could get a hearing and probably a result because of the disparity of sentences between Ahmed and myself. After such a long time, it was a relief. Feeling a burden lifted, I was able to get stuck in to the study of my college courses. The first counselling course I did was 'Christian Counselling', then 'Introduction to Psychology', followed by 'Introduction to Sociology', then 'Human Relations', and finally 'Pastoral Counselling'. I passed them all with high Bs. I was always busy and thoroughly enjoyed it all. My patience was sometimes close to snapping, but having so many good people around me who were always ready to listen really helped.

On 28th January 2000, my appeal was heard. I was not allowed to attend and I had to wait five days to hear the result. As expected, I received a reduction in sentence of two years. I felt that this was unfair because I had made my admission of guilt at the earliest opportunity. In addition, I was upset because the court would not hear my new evidence about Joe Roberts's involvement. Still, I was glad that I now had the chance of making parole on 18th December 2000. I applied for a D-cat status and was turned down by the South Five governor, but when I told him the news that I had received a reduction of two years, he changed his mind on the spot and granted my request. God was bringing many exciting changes.

The day came to do the speech at the Kairos weekend. I was very nervous to begin with but I soon got into it. I was determined that I would trust the Holy Spirit to help me, and that's what I did. The chapel was full of guests from many of the church denominations: Catholic, Methodist, Salvation Army and Pentecostal, Church of

England, Baptist and more. Beyond them, there was also the prison chaplain, a few military generals, a Home Office representative, the prison governor, the Mayor of Bury St Edmunds and many more. After all the new Kairos inmates had bravely got through some very moving speeches, I was asked to say the final word. My heart beat heavily as I walked to the front. I smiled and took a deep breath and cracked, 'Praise God' to many echoes of 'Amen'. I began to speak about the importance of prayer and how I had got through very difficult times with God's help. I talked about the many life stories I had read while in prison, and about meeting and praying with many of those authors. I had four of five of their books on hand to hold up to emphasise the point. Then I turned to the inmates sitting at the front and encouraged them about the importance of prayer and study of God's word, explaining that both had helped me so much. I related that life was much harder when I missed prayer and that it was so essential to keep the devil at bay. I told the audience that since all these men had arrived on Kairos, they had all undergone enormous change for the better and were now children of God. I smiled and roared a thank you, and then it was over. It all took about twenty minutes. Then there was a standing ovation. As I was quietly thanking God for helping me through this major step, I suddenly remembered my vision in Dartmoor three years earlier about standing in front of so many people speaking. Now it had happened, just as God had shown me, in spite of my unbelief. Who can say God is not real?

Even the officers came up to me and shook my hand afterwards but I protested that the speech they had heard was down to the Holy Spirit, and not me. It was God who had done all this! As I looked back through the years in prison, I could see God's hand on my life – teaching me slowly but surely.

Stewart Beaumont, the assistant chaplain, came back to work after a long illness. He was great to have around. A tall, kind man who always had time for everyone, he had a heart for all the inmates and worked so hard doing all he could to ease the suffering of needy men. Stewart was a trained counsellor and, together with Chaplain Mark Hunt, and the Catholic leaders Father Michael Teader and Sister Carmel, they talked and prayed with me each day and saw my inner problems come to the surface. Their prayers and patience played a big part in my healing and transformation. Such love is found in true Christians that have the Spirit of God in them.

As Father Michael and Pastor Stewart prayed with me one day, regardless of their respective denominations, God showed Michael – through a kind of mental picture – that I had built high walls of protection around myself. He said that he saw a little child inside who was afraid, and so he prayed that I would be restored.

All along the way in prison God put people there to help me to find healing for my deep scars, which needed a lot of patience. Not everyone can deal with helping someone with such scars, especially in a stubborn man as me. God has prepared many people to do just that, to comfort us, so that we in turn will be able to comfort others in the same way. This is what it says in 2 Corinthians 1:4.

There have been many who have concluded that I was a fool living in cloud-cuckoo-land for believing in God, but I know that it is they who are the foolish ones. The bravest thing I ever did was to step out of the flow and declare my faith in God.

Brian the preacher-man

Stewart encouraged me to prepare a sermon, or talk. I was reluctant at first because of my fear but realised that I had to continue to build on what I had already learned. I decided to give a sermon on prayer, and chose one that was given to me by Claud Trigger, my 86-year-old postal counsellor. He had sent some sermons to help me when I was studying the course 'Principles of Preaching'. The one that really excited me was 'Jabez and His Big Prayer'. In 1 Chronicles 4:9–10, there is a really short two-verse story about Jabez in the midst of a long list of names:

> Jabez was more honourable than his brothers. His mother had named him Jabez, saying, 'I gave birth to him in pain.' Jabez cried out to the God of Israel, 'Oh, that you would bless me and enlarge my territory! Let your hand be with me, and keep me from harm so that I will be free from pain.' And God granted his request.

This tiny nugget of biography inspired Claud to write a whole sermon about sixty years before, and so I decided to deliver the same talk myself. The day arrived and my heart was beating hard again but I took a deep breath and started slowly, praying silently for the Holy Spirit to take over. I had to cut it short to fit it into the time I had to speak. That day there were many new inmates in the chapel. During the sermon, I used all the skills I could remember from my lessons to reach the men. Eye contact, illustrations from real life, pausing at the key moments and so on. But most of all, I think they listened because I was an inmate just like them, and they were amazed by the fact that a fellow prisoner could speak to them in this way. Many approached me after the service to speak about where I had developed my faith. It was a very special day, thanks to Stewart Beaumont who encouraged me to do it.

Because I was now a D-cat prisoner, I could apply to go to an open prison. I knew that it would take some time. There were some jobs near Highpoint available for five inmates working outside in the community. Four took jobs in the forestry department, but the one position that I was drawn to was working with brain-damaged people. I was the only one who went for that job. These were people who had suffered from strokes, road accidents and so on. I applied and was assessed by my personal officer, Mr Palmer, and the wing governor. They both passed me with flying colours. It had taken so long to gain the people's trust and this was such good news for me that I cried for joy, thanking God for giving me this opportunity.

I shared with the chaplain that I wanted to work outside and he encouraged me that it was the best way forward. I had been working as the chapel orderly for sixteen months, and I thanked the chaplaincy team for all their help and encouragement. Finny replaced me as orderly. He had worked as chapel orderly at Dartmoor as well. God was also teaching him in a deep way and I remembered his frequent encouragement in Dartmoor. 'Training ground brother, training ground,' he would say when times were hard there.

Free . . . to a degree

I worked at Headway House in Bury St Edmunds for the next six weeks. My first duty, of course, was to make the tea. Then I would sit with patients and help them in art or woodwork classes. Taking them to the toilet was something that I was embarrassed about at first, but I soon realised that they needed me. 'There but for the grace of God go I,' I thought. I felt privileged to be able to work with these people and realised how life can change so quickly for many.

But it did not last for long. After six weeks, the Home Office decided to make cuts and stop funding the 'out workers', as our jobs were considered expensive. After that, I was out of work for two months. I found this hard, but something good was on the way. With my D-cat status, I was now eligible for 'town visits', which meant that I could go out for a day anywhere within a twenty-five-mile radius of the prison. I only had to find someone who could take me. My family lived far away in Wales, so I asked Dorothy, one of the prison chapel visitors who came along every week to the Sunday service. Dorothy was a well-spoken lady of about 70-years-of-age. One of her legs was in a brace, and gave her a lot of pain. She couldn't walk without it. She would come into the prison week in, week out and be a towering support to everyone. She was delighted when I asked her if she would be my chaperone, and we quickly decided that Cambridge would be a great place for a day out. Having been out in Headway House for a few weeks, I was used to some freedom, but that had been work and not play. Dorothy and I had a lot of fun visiting historic sites and churches.

We visited the Christian bookshop. I saw an excellent book by Dr E. K. Victor Pearce about how science is compatible with the Bible and Dorothy bought it for me. This was one of the books in a series called *Evidence for Truth*, and led the reader through an amazing amount of convincing scientific evidence that the Bible is true. I found that it helped me to strengthen my faith, and to understand even more about God's word. It was a top day out for Dorothy and me.

Just a few weeks later, my old friend Joshua came to see me from Holland with his girlfriend Monique and her son Dan. I was able to arrange for a town visit for the Saturday. It was fantastic to see them waiting by the gate, then to be able to join them and just drive off (although I was expected to return by 4 p.m. at the latest). I decided go to Cambridge again, as Joshua and Monique had never been there. We walked around the city, and then I ate the most succulent steak that I ever tasted! I had one pint of beer with the meal, which was another taste of freedom. I stopped for a split second and wondered as I drank: would I be able to let alcohol go when I was finally free? Would I have a problem with it? We got back to the prison on time and we said our goodbyes. My head was aching slightly because of the excitement of the day.

Dorothy took me out again a few weeks later and this time we went on a guided tour of Newmarket National Stud. It was a very interesting day out and we enjoyed it very much. However, with the pleasure of these away-days came an increased longing to be free again. I know that true freedom is in the heart and comes from God. I also know that many people out in the community feel like they are in their own prisons. Yet I had been locked up for so long that I wanted desperately to spread my wings.

My probation officer from Swansea came to interview me to make a report on my progress for the Parole Board. After that, it was the turn of the prison probation team at Highpoint, and then my personal officer Mr Palmer. They all made excellent reports, which I was later able to read. I was also allowed to add to my parole dossier whatever I thought was relevant to help me. By this time, I had collected references from all of the chaplaincy team, from the Kairos co-ordinator, and from the manager of Headway in Bury St Edmunds. I wrote a letter for the Parole Board and put my references in the dossier. I also added a report of all my ICI college progress. Now that I'd not had a job for two months, I'd had the time to myself to complete the fourth course for the counselling certificate.

News of a transfer came through and in no time I was on my way to Prescoed open prison, near Pontypool in Wales. I was going home again. I really felt sad at leaving the chapel on Sunday and was given a wonderful send-off by inmates and staff. Ten inmates put their hands on me and prayed for a God-blessed future. Even at the reception on the way out, the staff gave me a warm chorus of 'thanks for everything Brian, we'll miss you here.' It was a very touching and unusual way to leave a prison. I was certain that God had chosen for me to go there.

I had to get into a security van just like the one I was first taken to Swansea prison in, a tiny sweatbox. But I didn't care, because I was going home to Wales. It was enough that I would soon be seeing my brothers and sisters again. I was very excited.

TEN

Close to the gates

Here I was, halfway through my ten-year sentence, and hoping desperately for my release. Most drug smugglers don't get parole the first time they appeal to the Parole Board. I felt it was reasonable to expect freedom in December 2001, but I was hoping that, because of my hard work, I would get out in December 2000.

Meanwhile, here in Prescoed open prison, there were no fences. After checking into reception, I was shown to my cell and was handed a key to open and lock my door as I pleased. There were no 'lock-downs', even at night. The only restriction, it seemed, was that we were expected to be in our house blocks by 9.30 p.m.

In the morning, I got down to finding out about the computer courses that were available. First though, all new inmates had to be assessed for suitable work allocation. Some were sent to work on the farm with the cows or the pigs, and some went to the catering, cleaning or the maintenance and repairs department. I was sent to the farm even though I showed them all my hard work and pleaded that I wanted to learn about computers.

'You will go where we send you Morris,' ordered the allocation officer, Mr Edwards.

For the next three weeks, I was required to get up at 5 a.m. to fetch the cows from the fields, feed them and muck out their cowsheds. But then, after really going at it hard one day, my back gave me some problems and I told the doctor. He put me on the 'B' working list, which meant I was unable to do heavy work. Officer Edwards wasn't very happy, believing I had faked the problem to get off that job, but I wasn't too worried about that. I wanted to do well, and I was not prepared to do more damage to my back simply because of the system.

The next step was my risk assessment for home leave. Officer Powell called me into the office on the PA system and, fearing bad news again, I took a deep breath and walked in.

'I have been looking through your file and discovered that you haven't done any of the usual prison courses required for parole release,' he said. 'You'll never get parole with these religious courses Morris.' There was a mocking tone in his voice. 'But your record is very good with no adjudications.'

I wondered why he had not mentioned the adjudication for fighting in Swansea prison while I was on remand awaiting trial. I imagined that he couldn't have looked at all of my files yet. Two weeks later he called me into the office again. This time he was grinning like a Cheshire cat.

'I've discovered in your file that you were warned at HMP Dartmoor, Morris,' he exclaimed with a smirk. Had I forgotten about something, I wondered? Now what?

'You were given an official warning for holding Bible classes in your cell!'

He sounded triumphant. I was so relieved and glad to hear that this accusation was for doing God's work that I almost burst out laughing, but I just nodded, and wondered what happened to the file on my fight in Swansea. I am sure that God had a hand in it going missing! Officer

Powell had no alternative but to write a fully positive report.

Officer Edwards called me to the office and told me I could start in the woodcraft class. It had been twenty years since my carpenter's course in Holland, and I wasn't planning on using any of the machines because I was still afraid after the incident with the circle-saw back then. I was required to make some boxes and other small items. It was much better than farm labour, and my back soon got better. I still wasn't allowed into a full-time computer course, but there was a night class that I could attend from 6–8 p.m. I applied as soon as I could and started doing a beginner's computer course.

Where there was a will, there was a way. I was confident that I would get parole even though Officers Powell and Edwards were convinced I had no chance. I knew I had worked very hard for almost five years and felt sure that I would get it. Inmates are always advised to expect the worst – so that then anything better becomes a bonus, but somehow I couldn't do that. I was always an optimistic person when my hope was rooted in a living God.

One day I received a letter from Jamie, the big man who had become a Christian in my cell at Dartmoor the day I was turned down for Dutch repatriation. He wrote that he'd confessed to a murder, committed when he was fourteen. A woman had suddenly appeared during a burglary and he had panicked and hit her on the head. The next day he heard the news that she had died as a result. That day had haunted him ever since, and he'd carried this dark secret for all that time. Now, two-and-a-half years after he had given his life to Jesus, he felt the Holy Spirit was urging him to confess. He remembered how Finny had confessed at Dartmoor to previous crimes and felt that God was leading him to do likewise. He read out this verse, 1 John 1:9, before he confessed to the police: 'If we confess our sins, he is faithful and just and will forgive us our sins and purify us from all unrighteousness.'

I remembered how I had almost turned him away from my cell. In his letter to me, he had confided that it had been a very heavy burden to carry around with him for all those years, and it was a relief to unload it. The family of that poor woman would never have known what had happened and who was responsible, had Jamie not decided to follow Christ.

There were no Sunday church services at Prescoed, save for one or two irregular ones. It was the only prison I had been in that didn't have full Christian meetings. There were Catholic and Church of England clergy working there, but they had their own local parishes to care for as well. The Anglican vicar, Revd Peter Philips, was an encouragement to me even though he was not often there. His main work was with the sex offenders and vulnerable prisoners in the closed prison at Usk, four miles away. When I was running around Prescoed prison at night, I prayed for God to do a big thing there. I also asked God to restore regular services to Prescoed and save many there.

The big decision

One evening, I was called into the office by Officer Edwards, who handed me the following letter:

CRIMINAL JUSTICE ACT 1991: PAROLE NOTIFICATION

A panel of the Parole Board considered your application on 26th October 2000 and found you suitable for early release on licence, providing the terms of the release plan prepared for the Parole Board by your Field Probation Officer, together with any specific directions concerning release contained in the Parole Board's reasons, can be put in place. Parole may be withdrawn if the release arrangements agreed by the Board cannot be confirmed.

Additional Licence conditions

The Parole Board directed that your licence should include the additional condition(s) that you:

Comply with any requirements reasonably imposed by your supervising officer for the purpose of ensuring that you address your drugs problems.

Reasons

Mr Morris was convicted with another of the serious offence of knowingly importing a kilo of cocaine with intent to supply. His previous offences in this country were comparatively minor and committed thirty years ago. Reports indicate that, in prison, he quickly set about regaining control of his life by becoming drug-free and developing a pro-social value and belief system which should lead to an offence-free, positive lifestyle in future. He has behaved very well and seems highly regarded by all those with whom he has worked closely. He has had no adjudications. He has used his time constructively and gained qualifications which will prove useful in the future. He has worked his way steadily through the system and gained category-D status, as a result of which he has been working, without problem, in the community. Although he has done little offence-related work, it is felt that this can be undertaken with the Probation Service on release. His release plan is sound. All the above shows that much progress has been made. The panel considers that Mr Morris is now sufficiently low risk for early release on licence to be granted.'

I was beaming with an indescribable pleasure! It was literally the best news I had received in years. I had done my time well and was going home – praise God! Five years was a long time. I had lost my new family, my home of seventeen years, and all the personal belongings that I had accumulated over that time. I would not get the chance to travel until my licence expired in June 2003, and by that time nearly eight years would have passed. I knew that it would not then be wise to confuse my son who was being looked after by very special foster parents that I know God had provided. This meant that I had to let go and allow Sonny to grow up with his new family. I prayed to God and put it all in his hands. Who knows what will happen when Sonny has grown up and whether he will want to see me or not? All I know is that interfering too much in his life now will not help him at all. I must put his future and happiness before my feelings to be with him. I will always be there for him and decided that when I was finally allowed to travel again, I would simply ask the Child Care Agency if he wanted to see me.

While I was in HMP Highpoint, I had enquired about the possibility of going to Mattersey Hall Bible College to finish my degree in missions. I wrote to the Principal, but was told that they don't take newly released prisoners, and that they must first live in the community for two years before consideration. I felt bad about that because it meant that, although I had proved myself these past five years in prison, I now had to do it all over again in the free world. It seemed that the door was closed.

Instead, I applied to work with the Christian drug rehabilitation organisation Teen Challenge, and use what I had learned to help young people there. All I received from them though was an application form to go through their programme to help me off drugs! This was not what I needed – at least, not anymore. I wanted to work with them because I needed to learn the practical side of counselling.

I knew that Kerry Jenkins worked with Teen Challenge, and so I decided to wait to see if he would offer me a place with him. I felt that with his expertise as a counsellor, I could train with him voluntarily and become a counsellor myself. I had worked so hard to finish my own counselling certificate in time for my release. All I needed was the proper training.

I didn't think I was ready to go back to my hometown of Clydach to live, but the Probation Service in Swansea stipulated that this was what I must do. They had visited my brother John, his wife Angela and one of their sons Anthony, and they'd agreed to put me up for as long as was needed. Although I felt really grateful to them, this was far from ideal, as I was used to my privacy and would have to share Anthony's bedroom. But all that paled into insignificance when compared with the bigger picture – I was going to be allowed out, and I couldn't wait.

After six weeks at Prescoed Open, I was allowed to go on 'town visits' again for a day every weekend. Then, in November 2000, I was allowed 'home leave' for four days. The taste of freedom was wonderful, even if it was soured a little when I had to come back at the end. I thought of how I would settle in Clydach and I prayed to God for a place of my own. 'Lord, if you are sending me home, then please give me my own place to live in; I can't stay at John's for long. I have been five years locked up in a cell and I need some space.'

A few days later, when I phoned John to make arrangements for a town visit, he told me that an old friend of mine named Bryan had a flat for me if I wanted it. It was thirty yards from the house where I was born and a hundred yards from the Pentecostal church where Kerry Jenkins was pastor. I told John to tell Bryan that I would take it. I didn't have to look at it because I knew the street and every house on it! God had provided a home of my own even before I had got out. He was bringing me back to my roots. The promise, which was given to me at my baptism, that 'My God will supply all my needs,' was being proved absolutely correct. Not only did I have a private flat, but also a landlord who was a very good friend of mine. Bryan and I knew each other very well from school and grew into teenagers together. I couldn't ask God for more.

Each night I ran three miles on the path around the perimeter of the prison. I was really fit and ready for freedom. Drugs were now five years behind me, and I hadn't smoked for over three. I had prayed for those desires to leave me permanently, and miraculously they had. What I had been unable to achieve before on my own, God was more than able to do. I know that there are still areas of my life that need to change and improve, and I trust God that he will keep on chipping away until I am how he wants me to be. I felt like the clay pot that Jeremiah writes about: 'The pot he was shaping from the clay was marred in his hands; so the potter formed it into another pot, shaping it as seemed best to him' (Jeremiah 18:4).

We are living in a world that is increasingly wicked and I have been caught up in it by living a wicked life. I am glad that it was not just the police, but God who arrested me. Just like the Psalmist, David, acknowledged, all those years ago, 'He lifted me out of the slimy pit, out of the mud and mire; he set my feet on a rock and gave me a firm place to stand. He put a new song in my mouth' (Psalm 40: 2–3).

I was a new man, with new aims and a new vision – I wanted to tell others about God's love for them. That sly old dragon that had followed me around for so long needed to watch out now. God was turning me into a dragon slayer!

ELEVEN

Going home

The day I had looked forward to for so long was drawing near. I had now completed the Counselling, Assessment, Referral, Advice & Through-care (CARATS) programme run by Officer Brian Lewis at Prescoed, which would go some way towards complying with the conditions of my parole licence. With just a week to go before release, I was beginning to get 'gate fever'. I pictured myself being driven away in my brother's car for the very last time. I would not have to come back at the end of the day, or ever again, unless I was coming to bring the good news of Jesus to inmates or to encourage those who had already become Christians like myself in prison. Each day of that last week seemed to grow longer and longer, but finally the day arrived. I had accumulated quite a lot of things over the five years. There were so many things – study books, letters, papers, clothes, a guitar, a CD/cassette/radio, chopping boards and jewellery boxes that I had made in woodwork class – to carry, that I had to make three journeys to the reception to check out. Then it was another three journeys from the reception to the gate with even more stuff that had been stored in reception since my arrest.

My friend, Joshua, came from Holland to meet me at the gate. He had driven over in his camper van the night before and stayed with my brother Christopher. My eldest brother John and my sister in-law Angela were with him at the gate, obviously excited that I was at last coming home. I signed the ledger to confirm my release.

I was then handed a grant of £45 to last me a week or two as I went out into the free world – after five years in prison where the cost of my maintenance had been £90 a day. That's the system, which expects ex-offenders to get back into the 'normal' flow of society within the blink of an eye. The fact is that many re-offend and end up back in prison very soon after release. I think that if ex-offenders were freed a month earlier and given the money that would have been used to keep them in prison, they might just get a good start. Surely, there is a good chance that the ex-offender will revert back into a life of crime if he has no means of meeting his needs? But as for me, I was not worried about re-offending, because God had promised to supply all my needs, and I had learned that trusting God was far better than worrying. God sees the whole picture and the end from the beginning.

But what a day! I had my family, my church and friends there to support me, and I wanted to go and see them all. I was required to visit the probation officer straight from prison, however, so that's what I did first. There is an overwhelming urge to just let go when physical freedom finally comes. I wanted to get on a plane and go round the world without any restrictions and to have no one on my back, but there were two and a half years to go until my parole licence was up. Only then would I be allowed to finally travel. Yet, I had never felt freer in my life than in the last few years in prison, because Jesus Christ had set my heart free, and that is freedom indeed.

I was determined to use the time to write a book and learn more about computers. I could see now with hindsight that God had been preparing me for this task, with five years of writing thousands of letters, writing essays in my studies and the creative writing and journalism courses that I followed. The time came when I was bold enough to believe that I could write a book. I had read so many life-story books and thought that my own story might possibly help someone. God took the fear away and helped me take giant leaps of faith. I felt reassured, reading his word, that the lost years of my drug addiction would be restored. He promised to repay 'the years the locusts have eaten' (Joel: 2.25). My new life is built on God's promises now.

I had been a man of the world, but now I was a man of God because I believed in him who saved my life and gave me back my self-respect. Now I needed space to spread my wings. I had been shut up in such a small room for so long and felt like flying high in the sky like a bird. I asked God to make sure that I never even strayed slightly off the rails, for I knew there were more issues for me to work out in the free world. The frustration of having been locked up for so long had taken its toll, and Christians are not immune from frustration. It had been a very long, hard five years. God knows that I had given my best in trying circumstances. But I could do much better. I was aware that it was not hard work or my studies that had made me a Christian, but accepting Jesus as my King.

I had gained a comprehensive knowledge of God's word, and I was learning to trust his promises. This was something that was more sure and certain than anything I had before. I knew that God would 'never leave me, nor forsake me.' My faith in Jesus would carry me through. The freedom I needed was only physical; I was already free in my heart and it felt marvellous. The next few weeks were crucial in the continuation of my journey with God, and I was determined to keep praying and attending the church nearby.

I know very well that the Christian journey is never going to be easy and that people are ready to pull you down if you step out of line. I know too, from bitter experience, that when someone becomes a Christian, they don't suddenly become perfect and never sin again. But because I've sinned (done bad things) at times, it does not mean that I am a hypocrite. There are no perfect Christians. But I know that I must always do my best not to sin and as long as I give myself – wartish failures and all – to God, he will finish what he has started. I had been cleaned up a lot and I am still being worked on now. I don't want to do the things that used to hold me down anymore. My pride, lack of humility and impatience is still being dealt with. The big thing that has made the difference is my belief in Jesus Christ, and the assurance that he rose from death in order that I might be forgiven for all my evil and selfish ways. And I really do feel forgiven.

My Christian Counselling certificate arrived on the day I got out! It was the first post that I received at my brother's house. I had planned to finish my studies so that I would receive my certificate at the time of my release, but it was so special, miraculous even, that it had arrived on the very day I was released.

Outside

I was let out on the 18th December 2000, having served exactly 1,829 days. My 47th birthday was just three days later, and so I asked John to organise a coming home party. All my family in Clydach came and it was wonderful to let go and enjoy myself without the restrictions of prison life. I invited some old friends. One of them, Bryan Giles, a friend from my school and teenage years, approved of the 'new' Brian and had a very special birthday present for me – the key to my new flat. My first birthday in prison, a few days after my arrest, was the worst in my life. This one, a few days after I had left prison, was too good to be true. To be surrounded by all my family, who had forgiven me and wanted the best for me, filled my heart with joy and gratitude.

It was only a few days later that I started the decorating. John gave me all the paint, wallpaper and help I needed. My sister, Tina, gave me a three piece suite, two wardrobes, a dressing table and other things. My stay in John's house lasted two weeks and then I decided to spend some time with Chris. It was great to be with my brothers again. Chris helped me with painting the flat and did a great job, putting his heart and soul into it. We did the whole place out without missing an inch. John and Tina brought more furniture, clothes, kitchen utensils and a television. My sister Susan and husband Eric gave me a video recorder, bedspreads and many more goodies. My sister Wendy and my beautiful nieces, Donna and Hayley, gave me a mobile phone and a trendy jacket. My brother Carl and his wife Lynne gave me clothes, a stereo and many other things besides. Now I had a home ready to live in, a wardrobe full of new clothes and, most of all, my family back.

They were all delighted to see me home, twenty-five years after I had left with Noor for Holland. It felt great to be back, although I did not know how the locals would see it, and whether or not I would be accepted socially.

The church put out the word that I needed a double bed. They prayed, and lo and behold, God provided me with a double bed! A wonderful Christian couple, hearing about my need, got in touch with the church and offered me an almost-new bed – a swift answer to prayer! Then I bought an excellent single bed very cheaply and put it in my spare bedroom. Yes – I even had a spare room! I received chairs, linen, cutlery, pots pans, toasters, chip pan, grill, towels and more. Everything just kept pouring in and I felt that God was again proving the promise that he will supply all our needs and also restore what was lost and more.

The flat was situated at the back of a large house and was very quiet. I had experienced so much noise over the past five years that it was a special thing to be able to live in such a place. It was in a very peaceful road in Clydach, with no barking dogs, and there was a huge garden to work on when I got round to it. Financially, I was able to manage without worrying about needing more. Everything was being taken care of. The housing benefit paid my rent and community tax, and so I didn't have to worry about any bills that I couldn't handle. Bryan, my landlord, gave me a week's rent back because I had decorated the flat and, after a few attempts, I managed to get a grant from the Social Security for £333, which was all I needed for a second-hand fridge and gas cooker.

My new flat was really lovely; I had been blessed in so many ways. My brother Chris could hardly believe that I had got so much together in such a short time. He shifted nervously as I explained to him that it was God who was doing all this. It was not easy for me to mention God in my family. God was associated with mental cases – with people who had 'lost the plot'. I felt so sad to think that 'God' is a word that people feel embarrassed to talk about these days and that many don't want to hear about. Still, I continue to pray for my family and the local people that they will be able to come to know God as a father, friend, and king one day.

Joe Roberts, the man who had asked me to bring the drugs to Wales (and who I believe was partly responsible for me landing in prison) had moved out of Clydach by now. He made no attempt to come and see me to thank me for what I did for him in court. His brother Jerry has told me that Joe didn't want me to know where he lived. He has nothing to worry about. I don't hold anything at all against him and I would love it if he came to visit to talk things over so that we could clear the air. It is no longer necessary for him to go around ducking and diving, afraid of bumping into me. He could put the matter behind him and live in peace. One day, sooner or later, Joe and I will bump into each other and I will want to talk with him to reassure him that there's no need to worry. I would love to tell him about God and thank him for his part in my salvation. Perhaps instead, he will read this book and want to know more. I hope so.

I only know that I wanted to tell my story, warts and all. I stand by every word and have written it according to what I believe and know to be the truth. It is God who has prepared me so that I am able to write my story with its many twists and turns as I have described in this book. Having read my story, you may say that because of my life of crime I deserved the sentence I received. I agree. The main thing is, God had his way and caught me good and proper! I needed to get that twelve-year sentence in order for him to do his work in me – so that I would learn to rely on him more and more, to discover that when I trust him for all my needs, there is a far better future waiting for me than I could ever dream of (Jeremiah 29:11).

Rebuilding work begins

I decided to go to the Glamorgan Alcohol and Drug Abuse Centre to see if they would take on trainee counsellors. I left them my number, but they never got back to me. On the way to their centre, I discovered a Christian Counselling Agency and felt I just had to go in, where I was told that I could have an interview. I was so excited by this that I was convinced that I would receive some training there. The counsellor knew Kerry Jenkins and they had spoken on the phone about me. This made me very confident that I would be taken on.

Sadly, however, they told me they couldn't help me and I was really disappointed. Two or three years' training were needed to achieve an approved qualification. I hinted again to Kerry later that I would love to be invited to Teen Challenge to learn counselling skills with him, but I heard nothing more about this either. I really felt I had a lot to offer with all my experience. I was frustrated at first, but quickly realised how easy it was to forget that God was leading. I should be more patient; maybe he had something completely different lined up for me? I tried a different angle instead. I needed more computer training, so I applied for a City and Guilds Information Technology course in computing.

I started the City and Guilds computer course, and there was so much time available in between lessons that I decided to start writing my story. It seemed to me that God was leading me to begin, and presenting me with a wide open door. Everyone at the training centre encouraged me in the venture. I was, after all, learning about word processing as part of the course. It was a skill that I needed to catch up on if I was going to write a book, and I was really contented and relaxed when doing it.

Pastor Kerry asked me to tell my story at our church. I decided to phone the *Evening Post* and let them know about my speaking engagement, as I figured they might be interested. After all, I was the infamous front-page one-and-a-half-million pound 'drug baron' headliner in 1995 and 1996. I spoke to a journalist from the *Evening Post* and asked him if he was interested in doing an article on my talk. He agreed and an article was written after a telephone interview. The reason I called him was to attract more people to hear my story and to reassure the locals that I had changed. Another sign of God's goodness was that not one person in Clydach has said a bad word to me and I have been treated with respect and kindness. I gave the journalist Pastor Kerry's name to check it out. On the following Saturday, my story was in the *Evening Post*. 'Ex-Cocaine Smuggler Finds Faith', said the headline.

Quite a few of my family turned out to hear me speak, and I knew that the article in the *Evening Post* would help bring others too. Just as I had once dreamt, I was now standing at the front of Pastor Kerry's church! I probably did drag on a bit, but this was my day to show Clydach, my home, that God had done wonderful things in my life, and that he was taking a personal interest in my future.

Each week I had to visit the probation officer. After two months, it was reduced to once a fortnight and later to once a month. I also attended a weekly Narcotics Anonymous meeting (NA) to keep to the conditions of my licence.

Some old friends didn't want to get too close now that I had become a Christian. It seemed that they felt more comfortable with the old drug dealer and gangster that I had been. I felt that, deep down, they were glad for me, but were not ready yet for the big step that I had taken. I just prayed, and continue to pray, that they too will come to know Jesus Christ. I must say also, though, that I have gained many more new friends as a Christian. I believe in a big God, an awesome God just like Jabez did in the passage that I'd preached my sermon on. He prayed and received what he asked for. I am praying for all my family and many people in Clydach and elsewhere to know the truth of Christianity, and I believe that God will answer in ways that will continue to surprise me.

I am very thankful to the Prison Fellowship for all their support and love while I was in prison. After my release, I continued to attend their monthly meetings. When I was held in Swansea prison on remand I had promised to tell my story at one of their meetings when I was free. Mel and Anne, two Christian friends, were able to give me a lift to the first meeting I attended. On the way there, I mentioned that I wanted to write a book about my life but I needed a computer. Straight away, they suggested that before we went in we should pray about it. Anne just said, 'Please Lord, give Brian a computer to write his story.'

And God heard our prayer. After telling my story, a man came up to me and said that if I wanted a computer to write a book about my story, he had one that I could have. How about that for answered prayer? After experiences like this, I cannot doubt that God is mighty real indeed! Some people say that you cannot 'prove' that God is real, but I believe that he has proved himself over and over to me. I had not mentioned in my talk that I needed a computer, and had only said that I was planning to write my story. Since that day, I have been writing enthusiastically, as I hope you can tell.

Used by God

There is still much more to change in my life and I know that God is still working on this rough diamond. I did not receive an instant 'cure' when I gave my life to Jesus. The healing process is ongoing. I believe that my life has changed dramatically since I started to follow him. I admitted my guilt and said sorry; I believed that Christ was raised from the dead, and asked him for help by inviting him into my heart to rebuild my life. He answered me, clearly and powerfully. I now know beyond a shadow of a doubt that everlasting life is available to anyone who believes in Jesus.

I was invited to more and more speaking engagements and felt God using me to help others. Kerry drove us up to London for the Alpha course conference and I was able to introduce him to the Alpha prison team who I had met in prison and had come to know and love. We had a fantastic time staying with friends in London and enjoyed the vibrant worship at Holy Trinity Brompton.

After coming back to Swansea I was asked to speak at the 'Inside Outside' conference in Swansea. This was a conference bringing together various Christian prison groups for the initiating of a new 'Community Chaplain.' His name was David Emery, and he was a Salvation Army Major who would liaise between the prison chaplain of HMP Swansea, churches and local services to help settle ex-offenders successfully back into the community on release. I was chosen as one of four main speakers alongside HMP Governor Vicky O'Dea, the prison chaplain Revd Lionel Hopkins and David himself. There was also a surprise speaker – The Rt Hon. Donald Anderson, MP for Swansea East! How could I, an ex-offender, ever have imagined speaking alongside such people? And to top that day off, the whole time I was sitting next to a lovely elderly gentleman who I got on very well with and later discovered was a High Court judge! Is that just chance, or signposts that restoration and transformation were happening to me in a big way? As I have stated repeatedly, my God is awesome!

After the conference, I managed to talk to Vicky O'Dea and told her about how I wanted to come into the prison to speak to the inmates, but because I was still on licence, was not allowed to do so.

'I decide who comes into my prison Brian,' she smiled. 'You leave it with me, and I'll get back to you.'

I had to be patient, but five months later I received a letter from HMP Swansea allowing me to attend under supervision of the chaplaincy team.

Now I have the rare privilege of being able to go, as a free man, onto the wings I used to be held on and talk with inmates.

I was also asked to speak at a school concert, which was packed full of young people. Every one of them listened intently and cheered heartily at the end, with many coming up to me afterwards to find out more about my story and how God had changed me.

Our Prison Fellowship group asked me if I would like to travel to Swanwick, near Nottingham, with group leader Jane Morgan for PF's biannual conference, and I jumped at the chance. It took a few hours to drive to Swanwick and by the time we'd arrived, freshened up and found the dinner hall, it seemed that we were the last people in, and we were led to a table at the back. On the way through the tables, at least five people said hello to me and asked what I was doing there.

Later I met up with many of the prison visit teams I had met in Dartmoor and Highpoint. I had that sense of belonging again and everyone was overjoyed at seeing each other after all this time. The last time I had seen many of these wonderful people I was in jail. Now I was involved in the same work as them, and I felt like I belonged.

We got back home refreshed and buzzing with excitement after being encouraged to get more involved in Christian prison work. We began to realise that the work we did with inmates would be like the ripples on a pond that spread on and on after a splash. But we also realised that this comes at personal cost: if we were to be effective in our work with hurting people, we needed to be close to God ourselves. It is necessary for a Christian to spend regular time praying, alone and with others, and to get stuck in to the Bible, the word of God. In order to be useful to God, we must stay close to him, so that we might remain protected from the devil's sly temptations. Otherwise, it does not take the human mind long to be persuaded to return to former ways.

The City and Guilds computer applications course came to an end, and out of thirty students, I was asked if I would like to take part in a pilot scheme for a course called European Computer Driving Licence (ECDL). The men running the course were Christians, and I just knew that God had caused them to ask me. Everyone knew about my criminal record and there were others who I thought would have been asked first. I jumped at the chance and worked hard, finishing it and passing all the exams in three months.

I applied for a number of jobs again, but was unsuccessful, so I decided to stick with learning computer skills

for the time being rather than do nothing. I started studying for diplomas in two- and three-dimensional
Computer Aided Design (CAD) and completed both
courses, again passing all my exams.

Then, when that was finished, I tried for various jobs
but was politely turned down or received no reply from
them all. I wasn't going to panic though, because I knew
that God was in control.

I was asked again to speak, this time in Redruth,
Cornwall, at a Prison Fellowship meeting, with all
expenses paid. An ex-offender like myself, the area group
leader Brian Tramaine had invited me there out of the
blue. It was six months since we'd met at the Prison
Fellowship conference, and I had forgotten about Brian,
but clearly he had not forgotten me. I had a wonderful
time with him and his wife Margaret. They had a surprise
for me too. A Christian officer who had worked for many
years in HMP Dartmoor, and who I knew from my time
there, had also been asked to come and speak. It was an
unlikely affair, with both ex-con and ex-screw sharing the
same stage and sharing Jesus.

I was beginning to wonder about how I could pay for a
trip to Holland to see my son, should the chance arise. I
was not earning enough money to be able to save up for
it, so I prayed and left it in God's hands. Then, in April
2003, I received news that my book had been accepted for
publication. I had worked so hard on my story for such a
long time that it was a great relief. Since the day when I
received my computer I'd always known in my heart that
it would be published, and once again God had come
through for me. I just knew it was an answer to prayer for
the money I needed to go to Holland. A matter of trust

again! 'God's got it all under control, Brian boy,' I muttered to myself out loud. 'Learn it, and keep it in your heart.'

Going back

Then the job that I had wanted to do all along came up, and I was reminded again that I needed to learn more patience. An organisation called the Rainbow Group ran two 'life-controlling problem rehabs' near Swansea, and one was only twenty minutes away from me by bus. They needed volunteers and I applied and was accepted. It was something I felt I could help a lot with because of what I had been through. I knew I could empathise with those hurting men, and hoped that it could lead to full-time work.

A week later, I reached the end of my probation period, having successfully attended every appointment with my probation officer without any hitches in two and a half years.

At the start of June 2003 I received an email from Prison Fellowship asking if I could return to Highpoint to speak to the inmates who were about to finish their Compass course (the new equivalent to the Kairos course). I could hardly wait to return and be reunited with many of the wonderful people I'd met there.

When I got off the train at Cambridge, Dorothy (now 79), was waiting to take me to my lodgings for the night. It was great to see her smiling face again. She took me to Roy, one of Highpoint's other volunteer Christian workers. I had spoken to Roy many times when I was chapel orderly at Highpoint and he had become a great encouragement to me.

The next morning we arrived at the gate with the tall razor-wired fence surrounding the huge modern buildings. There had been more wings built since I'd left, and they now held over a thousand inmates including women. Revd Mark Hunt, who I had come to know so well during my sixteen months there, was on hand to greet me. The first thing I wanted to do was pray with him.

I sat and marvelled at what was happening in my life. I had seen many people come in to share their stories and now I was going to share mine – the wheel had come full circle. I felt honoured and privileged and when ten offenders walked into the room I got up to shake their hands, although many of them were looking bored at the prospect of yet another Christian lesson. They had been on the project for about six months and would graduate in a week's time. Paul, the pastor running the Compass project, introduced me as we sat down in a circle on the easy chairs that I had moved around the room hundreds of times. After I had explained who I was and that I was as familiar with the prison as they were, they seemed to sit up and listen to my story. I had been where they had been, and that meant I had credibility. I relaxed and the words poured out of my mouth about how God had changed my life, and about the trials and learning that had taken place. When I finished, I received a round of applause and a cheer. I realised again that this work was made for me. The way that God was touching these men through what I was saying to them gave me a warm glow inside.

Sonny day

It was June 2003, and I was very excited. The foster family who were looking after Sonny Ray in Holland had contacted me to say that I could come to visit my son in July. This meant that I would see him for the first time since he had been two months old. He had only seen a few photos of me and I of him, and I knew that we wouldn't know each other. I thought through how I should behave in this strange situation, and decided that I must not be serious and emotional with him. Instead I just needed to remember to tell him that I loved him, and share something about my relationship with Jesus. I knew that Jesus would be with us both when we met, and so I left the whole situation in his hands, because in the Bible he said I should 'cast all my cares on him'.

I was swimming between five and ten kilometres a week to keep fit and I would arrive a very different man to the Brian Morris who left Holland as a junkie seven and a half years earlier.

Finally, after excruciatingly slow-moving days of waiting, I touched down in Holland after nearly eight years away. My brother Ray picked me up at the airport. We had a great reunion and I felt immediately at home again as we drove through the Dutch countryside. I slept well that night. I made my way in the morning to the street in which I had lived for seventeen years before my arrest. I had heard that the whole street had been demolished, but when I turned into the Noorderbeekstraat, one side was completely rebuilt and half of the other side was still standing. My flat was still there! I walked past feeling a little strange, but definitely glad that I was not living there anymore. My net curtains were still hanging there too! It was empty. I walked quickly on and said to myself that all this was behind me now, and turned the corner.

The next morning Raymond took me to Leiden to meet my son. My heart was pounding with anticipation. Seven and a half years had passed since I last saw Sonny Ray. I waited in the meeting room, which had fresh coffee and kids' drinks on the table and a big box of toys in the corner. The social worker explained that I had to stay calm and just let Sonny come to me in his own time. She left the room to bring the family in. My eyes were fixed about three feet up the door – I wanted to see his very first reaction. Then, Sonny came into view, leading the family into the room. Our eyes met, and we both beamed with pleasure. There was only happiness between us. We relaxed immediately and hit it off right away. We had a truly wonderful hour and a half together, all in Dutch of course.

When I was helping Sonny to colour in a picture I asked him if he could speak any English, and he replied, 'I love you'. I almost let my tears gush out, but smiled, hugged him and simply said 'I love you too my boy'. It was a perfect end to the short time we'd spent together.

Sonny was still grinning with delight as we entered the lift together, and we promised each other we would write and keep in touch. Outside we waved our goodbyes, and I watched a very happy family disappear out of sight. Even though I had lost Sonny through my mistake-ridden past, and could have completely ruined his life, God has given him a very special love through this wonderful, loving family and I have the assurance in my heart that my son could not be in safer hands.

Forever a dragon slayer!

I began my story telling of how I thought I had simply been 'chased by the dragon', but in reality he'd held me in his grip. Now that I belong to Jesus Christ, the Lamb of God, I know that 'the dragon, that ancient serpent, who is the devil or Satan' (that's what the Bible calls him) will never give up trying to ensnare me with all kinds of temptations and distractions. That's his mission you see, to be as evil and destructive as God is loving and good.

You can be sure that when you are a Christian the battle for you will increase. But Jesus defeated Satan by dying on the cross, and was raised from the dead so that all who believe in him might live forever. The Bible says: 'For God so loved the world that he gave his one and only Son, that whoever believes in him shall not perish but have eternal life (John 3:16).

These are words that give life, and which have drastically changed my life. I believe them with all my heart, because I have seen the power of God at work before my eyes.

I have come to the end of this book, but I know that this is not the end of my story. Who knows what exciting chapters remain, for my God is a God who does wonders – in fact, he is an awesome God. I believe he is going to continue to enlarge my borders, just as he did for Jabez.

So may I ask a personal question? In these dark days that we live in, I believe that there exists an inherent hunger for the truth in every human being. Would you rather believe in your own 'truth', or even in some fashionable philosophy, or would you rather find out about the real 'truth' – Jesus Christ? Everyone has access to God through Jesus. He is only a prayer away, and it really is that simple.

At many points during my prison life, people came to see me to ask how they could get to know God. In each case I took them through the five steps below, which are taken from the Bible, and then asked them to say a prayer. That prayer is like the key that unlocks the door to Christ. Believe me when I say this: if you open that door to him, you will never ever want to close it again. So now, it's over to you.

There are five steps of Salvation:

Step 1: Acknowledge that you are a sinner (Romans 3:23).

Step 2: Recognise that God did something about it (John 3:16).

Step 3: Receive Christ as your Saviour (Romans 6: 23).

Step 4: Confess sin and get rid of it (1 John 1:9).

Step 5: Confess and believe Jesus is Saviour and Lord (Romans 10:9–10).

Here's a prayer for you to say if you want to:

Dear Lord,
I know that I have sinned against you and against others and am sorry.
I believe in my heart that you sent your Son to die for me on the cross.
Please come and live in my heart and be my Saviour; I receive you now.
I turn away from sin and ask that you help me to do this.
I confess with my mouth that Jesus is my Lord and Saviour and believe in my heart that he rose from death.
Thank you Lord for saving me,
Amen.

And if you've just said that prayer, then welcome to the dragon slayer's adventure, and God bless you!

Here is a poem by Vernon Charlesworth that I think fits in with my story and really spoke to me when I read it. I wonder what kind of reaction it will produce in you?

Men don't believe in a devil now,
As their fathers used to do;
They reject one creed because it's old
For another because it's new.

There's not a print of his cloven foot,
Not a fiery dart from his bow
To be found in the earth or air today!
At least – they declare it is so!

But who is it that mixes the fatal draught,
That palsies heart and brain,
And loads the bier of each passing year,
With it's hundred thousand slain?

But who blights the bloom of the land to-day,
With the fiery breath of hell?
If it isn't the devil who does the work,
Who does? Won't somebody tell?

Who dogs the steps of the toiling saint?
Who spreads the net for his feet?
Who sows the tares in the world's broad field?
Where the Saviour sows His Wheat?

If the devil is voted not to be,
Is the verdict therefore true?
Someone is surely doing the work
The devil was thought to do.

They may say the devil has never lived,
They may say the devil is gone,
But simple people would like to know
Who carries the business on?   *Vernon Charlesworth*

Brian's Prayer

Show me the way oh Lord so that I may know where to go.
Hear my cry for understanding of your wonderful grace.
Lead me along the road that leads to heaven.
Fill my heart with love and compassion,
As a human I am limited in strength.
That's why I need your wise guidance.
Fill me with your consideration for others,
So that I may share with them the lasting happiness you
provide.
Amen.

EAST END TO EAST COAST

Martin Saunders

An unlikely traveller.
An incredible journey.

When journalist Martin Saunders met champion weightlifter Arthur White, he had no idea what was around the corner. Arthur is a member of Tough Talk, a group of ex-hardmen from London's East End, whose lives have been radically and powerfully changed, and who now travel the world telling their stories.

Over the following six months, Martin hit the road with Tough Talk, following them from the picturesque mountains of France to the streets of a wounded New York. Along the way he uncovered countless amazing, shocking and amusing stories, made a few new friends, and watched as many lives were changed forever.

East End to East Coast is a book like no other. Part biography, part comedytravelogue, it charts the story of this amazing journey, while also asking some serious questions about masculinity and meaning.

ISBN: 1-86024-276-6   **Price: £5.99**

DAVID STREET'S CHRISTMAS DIARY

Martin Saunders

David Street hates Christmas.

He hates the food, the music, the parties, and the television. And he especially hates the eight-foot dancing Santa on his neighbour's front lawn. Three painful Christmases have made him dread the big day – with the spectre of another pushing him away from the daughter he loves and towards the depths of depression.

It looks like being another desperate December. But the arrival of a blank diary on his doorstep could just change everything. Will David learn to find some meaning among all the materialism? Or will he suffer another Christmas of bad memories and broken dreams?

ISBN: 1-86024-439-4   **Price: £2.99**